WRITING FOR
DECISION MAKERS

SECOND EDITION

WRITING FOR DECISION MAKERS

Memos and Reports with a Competitive Edge

SECOND EDITION

Marya W. Holcombe

Judith K. Stein

VNR VAN NOSTRAND REINHOLD
_____ New York

To our clients, from whom we have learned much.

Van Nostrand Reinhold
115 Fifth Avenue
New York, New York 10003

Chapman & Hall
2-6 Boundary Row
London SE1 8HN, England

Thomas Nelson Australia
102 Dodds Street
South Melbourne, Victoria 3205, Australia

Nelson Canada
1120 Birchmount Road
Scarborough, Ontario M1K 5G4, Canada

16 15 14 13 12 11 10 9 8 7 6 5 4

Library of Congress Cataloging-in-Publication Data

Holcombe, Marya W., 1944–
  Writing for decision makers.

  Includes index.
  1. Business report writing.   I. Stein, Judith K.,
1935–   . II. Title.
HF5719.H64   1987   808'.066658   86-24700
ISBN 0-442-23268-3

CONTENTS

PREFACE
TO THE
SECOND EDITION

The first edition of *Writing for Decision Makers* was successful because it met a real need of managers for a *system* for preparing a logical, persuasive argument for a particular audience. We continued to develop our thinking about that process as we worked with clients, and *Presentations for Decision Makers* was the product, in part, of that development. But concepts are never fixed in stone, and we have refined that process further, making it even easier to learn to "think before you write" and to translate that thinking into crisp, riveting words on paper.

Most of the material in the first six chapters of this second edition is new. We've also added new examples throughout and provided a note on writing electronically. In other words, this book is as current and practical as we can make it. We hope you both enjoy it and gain from it.

PREFACE
TO THE
FIRST EDITION

Demands on your time as a manager are endless, and you're often competing with others for support for your plans, ideas, and objectives. You realize that writing quickly, efficiently, and forcefully is essential to making the best use of your time and gaining that support. So you've picked up this book — a bit skeptically, because you've tried others with similar titles, and they've offered you only a rehash of eighth-grade grammar and a few hints about creativity and outlining. *This book is different.* We wrote it because we feel that by applying the managerial skills you already have to your writing, you can improve your reports and memos almost instantly and gain the competitive edge you need.

You will find very little grammar in this book. Instead, we show you how to plan, organize, and present your thoughts on paper in a way that will produce results. Each chapter tells you how to attack a step in the writing process:

- Identifying and focusing on the reader
- Solving the problem
- Planning your argument and drawing a picture of it
- Writing exciting and useful beginnings and endings
- Writing the first draft
- Adding visuals
- Revising
- Making the document attractive

There is also a unique chapter on helping others to write better by effectively appraising their writing and on editing and reviewing for superiors, sensitive tasks often neglected in management writing books.

We've included dozens of examples of managers' writing to show you the improvements that result when our techniques are applied. Checklists and guidelines will enable you to recognize and remedy your own particular writing weaknesses. You'll find that once you've learned a few simple rules, you can use this system for any kind of writing you do on the job — letters, memos, reports, and speeches. We are convinced that reading this book and practicing its lessons will prove to you that good managerial writing is not an inborn talent, but a skill that can be learned and put to your competitive advantage.

ACKNOWLEDGMENTS

The first edition of this book was, in large part, the result of the support and intelligent guidance of two of our colleagues at the Yale School of Organization and Management: Larry Isaacson and Dennis Perkins. In addition, Art Bulger, Earle Kazis, Alan Koss, and Dave Kramer helped enormously by reading drafts of that manuscript.

The second edition owes much to our associates at Strategic Communications: Lalana Green, Jacalyn Diesenhouse, Brenda Duffy, and Susan Anderson. Lalana Green's insights and disciplined reading contributed immeasurably to the final version of chapter 8, and we'd like to give her special thanks.

The data for the Budget Finance case were kindly provided by Stanley Kanney. The information is accurate, but the names of people and organizations have been changed.

THE MANAGERIAL APPROACH TO WRITING

If you feel you're spending too much time writing reports or memos that get ripped to shreds, or if you can't understand why your writing doesn't get you what you want, don't blame your English composition teacher. Business writing requires entirely different skills. If you've heard that "all good writing is editing," and you don't know how to parse a sentence, don't give up. Correct grammar and usage are important, no question about it, but even more important is the thinking you do before you write; and you can learn how to think strategically.

We know that good communicators ask themselves specific questions about the recipients of any communication in order to decide what and how much to say. They may, if they are intuitively good communicators, ask the questions subconsciously. But among the people with whom we've worked, even the best communicators have found that understanding the process of putting together a good presentation — written or spoken — helps them do the job better and faster. That's what this book is all about. It will show you a system for developing a logical, persuasive argument (defined as "a course of reasoning" not a "disagreement") and for converting that argument into a well-written, attractive document (see exhibit 1-1). The beauty of the system is that it is the same whether you

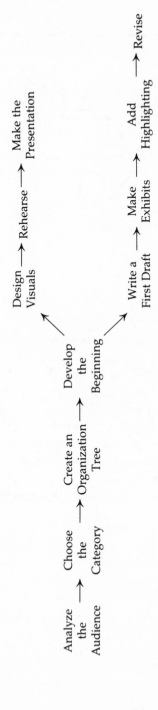

Analyze the Audience → Choose the Category → Create an Organization Tree → Develop the Beginning

Design Visuals → Rehearse → Make the Presentation

Write a First Draft → Make Exhibits → Add Highlighting → Revise

Exhibit 1-1. The process of putting together your ideas is the same whether you are writing or speaking.

are going to write or speak, whether the news is good or bad, whether you are recommending change or telling someone how to do something. What you will learn from this book will help you any time you communicate.

The first part of the system is the thinking part. Before you actually write paragraphs, you will know exactly what you want to say. You will thus avoid false starts and cut-and-paste sessions. You should be able to produce a finished memo or report in one-and-a-half drafts.

The approach you will learn in this book is different from traditional approaches to writing, and you will want to work through the whole process in order to understand how the parts fit together. Nonetheless, it is a good idea to have some sense of what you want to improve before you begin, so you will know what you've gained at the end.

Setting Goals

When we give writing workshops, we always ask: "What's the one thing you want to get out of this workshop?" And we generally get a long wish list. Perennial favorites include:

I want to organize my thoughts better.

I want to stop procrastinating.

I want to write more concisely.

I want to create meaningful graphs and charts.

I want to sell my ideas on paper.

'I want my writing to sound like me, not a computer.

I want to avoid endless rewriting.

and, among upper-level managers,

I want to help my people write better so that I can get the information I need to make decisions.

You've probably got a few additions of your own for the list. Most people have a pretty good idea of what they'd like to improve.

Exercise

To add some precision to your goals, try this: Pull out the last three or four short memos you've written and use them to answer the questions in the Writing Checklist. (Don't select memos that someone else has commented on for this exercise. Although the points may be telling, most people are more successful when they set their own goals rather than responding to punitive editorial comments.)

WRITING CHECKLIST

	Yes	No	Not Sure
1. Did this memo get the results you wanted?	____	____	____
2. Is this memo directed to the decision maker? Does it take into account his or her management style, his or her concerns?	____	____	____
3. Do you tell the reader, within the first few sentences, what the main point is, why the reader should care what you're saying, and how you are going to develop the rest of the memo?	____	____	____

4. Can you, by skimming the headings, understand the logic of the memo? ———— ———— ————

5. If you used charts and graphs, does each one make one point (and can you tell what that point is from the heading)? ———— ———— ————

6. If you were the reader, would you have a positive impression of the writer? ———— ———— ————

7. Do you write comfortably on a personal computer or word processor? Are you successful using an electronic mail system to send messages? ———— ———— ————

Your "no" and "not sure" answers will give you some clues as to where you think you could improve. Work through the chapters that deal with those areas especially carefully.

Question 1. Did you get the results you wanted? Getting people to do what you want them to do is a large share of management, and it's not easy. This whole book deals with getting results from a written communication. Chapter 2 relates to the broad strategic issues involved in getting agreement on an idea.

Question 2. Is this memo directed to the decision maker? Chapter 3 provides a reader profile that will ensure that you meet the needs of the right person.

Question 3. Do you tell the reader almost immediately your main point, why he or she should care about it, and how you're going to proceed? In part, this is covered in chapter 6, on beginnings and endings, but in a larger sense the chapters on organizing a logical and persuasive argument (chapters 3, 4, and 5) lead up to it.

Question 4. Can you follow the logic of the argument by skimming the headings? Chapter 8 deals with making the document attractive, which includes headings; but the chapters that helped you with Question 3 help you with this as well. If you've got a logical organization, you can construct sensible headings — automatically.

Question 5. Does every graph and chart make one point only, and can you tell what that point is by looking at the heading? Good exhibits help ensure that your message will be understood and remembered. Chapter 8 provides models of effective tables, charts, and graphs and gives you help in selecting those that support your argument.

Question 6. If you were the reader of this memo, would you think positively of the writer? The way you write can make you seem natural, competent, and precise, or stiff, unprofessional, or careless. Chapter 7 gives you concrete help in making your tone, word choice, and style reflect the kind of person you really are.

Question 7. Do you write comfortably on a personal computer or word processor? When you use electronic mail do your messages achieve their goals? A Note on Writing Electronically gives you insight and aid on communicating in the office of the 1980s.

How to Use This Book

Any intelligent, motivated manager can figure out how to apply general principles to his or her own writing assignments. But your goal is to learn the fastest way possible. So we've included two sets of exercises, one set based on the case studies in appendix 1, and one set for you to use with your own *current* writing assignments. At this point, forget about what you've done in the past. We don't want you to look at old memos and reports, restructure them, or — heaven forbid — edit them. Pick something you have to write within the next two weeks — the more substantial the better — and use that to work through the exercises.

Keep in mind that any time you write, you are trying to persuade someone of something. If nothing else, you want to persuade a reader that your view of the world is appropriate. Most often as a manager, however, you are writing to recommend a specific course of action. Therefore, you will be best served if you choose to work on a memo in which you must recommend a change or evaluate options.

If you're new on the job, or new to management, or a business school student, read quickly through the cases in the appendixes and pick the one that most appeals to you to work through the system.

If you can, find a friend or associate to work through the book with you. Many people like to lock themselves in a room and learn on their own. That's fine. But if you can find someone to work with you, you'll be ahead: You'll have your own version of Napoleon's corporal, who, rumor had it, Napoleon used to test his orders. If the corporal, who was not involved in making decisions, understood the orders, Napoleon assumed the generals would understand them as well. The hallmark of effective management writing is its content. If you work with another person, you'll each know whether you're getting your point across to someone else. Working as a team will also give you both valuable practice in helping others improve their writing, the subject of chapter 10.

As you work through this book, you'll be able to see improvement. You'll notice a change almost immediately, and by the end you will have made our system for effective writing a habit. Your first step is to learn techniques for assessing the strategic implications of writing things down, the subject of chapter 2.

2

WRITING STRATEGICALLY — THINK BEFORE YOU DECIDE TO WRITE

This whole book advocates thinking before you write, rather than writing in order to know what you think, which is a waste of management time. When you are communicating because you want to, rather than because you've been asked to, there are two distinct parts to the thinking process: <u>understanding the way things get done in your organization</u>, in order to know whether to advance your idea, and <u>preparing a specific communication</u>. In this chapter you'll learn to:

- Analyze your motives
- Test your ideas for feasibility
- Check your timing
- Recycle, if necessary, and try again

The process of getting what you want is by no means linear. At each step you have an opportunity to recycle and try again (see exhibit 2-1).

Step 1. Be Clear about Your Purpose   *don't complain or brag on paper*

Start with yourself. Do you want to change something or are you just complaining (or saying "Look at how great I am")? Neither

9

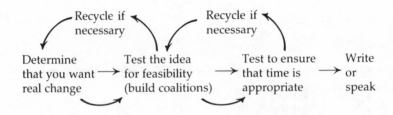

Exhibit 2-1. *The process of getting what you want is not linear.*

complaining nor bragging look very attractive in print (there's a place for both elsewhere, but that's a different book).

Step 2. Test for Feasibility *build coalitions*

Let's say you really do want to change something. You see a problem that begs to be solved, or you see an opportunity to improve the way things work. What's your first impulse? Hide in a corner, work out all the details, and spring it on the boss when he's alone? True, that way no one else will get the credit. However, for there to be any credit, the decision maker has got to "buy in," and the strategy we just outlined is almost certainly doomed to failure. Why? Because for any major change, unless you've involved other people who are knowledgeable or in a position to influence the decision maker, you simply won't know enough to make the strongest possible case for your idea. Consulting other people will give them an opportunity to buy in (politicians call this co-opting people) and give you the information you need to make a convincing case.

The same concept applies even if you are the boss. Authority just isn't what it used to be, and the people who work for you have many ways of sabotaging plans they don't agree with. If you involve them early on, you'll have a much better chance of getting their cooperation.

What if, when you mention your idea to a co-worker, it gets shot down or criticized? If you're like most people, you hate criticism. But you should always expect some resistance. Some people feel it's their obligation to play devil's advocate. Others may be jealous. Still others will try to protect their turf (for example, they may suspect that your idea will take money away from their department in the short run).

Look at it this way: Feedback on your idea, even negative feedback, is a vital source of information. Critics can tell you that similar ideas fell flat in the past — and they can tell you why those projects failed. You can then avoid, or at least circumvent, a particular land mine when you propose your idea. Furthermore, as the gurus of sales training say, objections can help you more than indifference or even lukewarm support. First, people have to care to object, ←︎ and if you can answer their objections, they may be your firmest supporters in the future. Second, people who express no opinion ←︎ or respond with polite murmurs of enthusiasm either don't understand what you're getting at (in which case, you should pursue the matter until they do) or they don't feel it will affect them either way (in which case, they won't actively support you). People who don't understand or don't care won't be your allies when it counts. At this stage, you are building coalitions. Without a coalition, you are unlikely to bring about any major change.

Step 3. Make Sure the Timing's Right

(If opposition is too strong, beat a retreat.) Perhaps the idea needs modifying, or perhaps the timing just isn't right (there have been rumors of an acquisition, the bottom just fell out of the stock market, the decision maker has other things on his or her mind). But don't be too quick to trash your project. Simply by talking to people, you've gotten them involved on some level. Not only that, but you've established relationships that can help you later when you decide to relaunch your proposal. Remember, it takes months, if not years, to get anything major adopted. To get a proposal off the ground, you need patience and persistence — and the recognition that nothing is ever totally lost, unless you let it go.

takes time; patience; persistence

Step 4. Consider Trying Again

Managers who have been with an organization a long time can fall into the trap of assuming that their counterparts will react according to an etablished pattern. But people change and so do their priorities. If you are convinced an idea is good, give it another try, ask more questions, and rebuild your coalitions — learning as you go. In particular, ask people to give specific reasons why they support your proposals — indications that they think they'll gain a major reward or avoid a risk of some kind. People do things for *their* reasons, not for yours, and they never do anything simply because it's for "the good of the company," even though they may say that. Be sure they have good reason to support you.

Once you've decided your idea has merit, the timing's right, you have support, and you know where the major concerns and objections are, you're ready to construct a logical, persuasive argument for your point of view. Remember, the first part of the process is the thinking part, so don't put clean paper in the typewriter. Start with some ~~scratch paper~~. To persuade anyone of anything, you must put your ideas forward in terms that are meaningful to that person. The pitch you make to the operations folk won't work with the financial folk. What you should know about your audience and how to find out is the topic of chapter 3.

SUMMARY

Before you plunge ahead with any idea, you should:

- Decide what you want to achieve
- Talk to people; be sure the idea makes sense to others
- Make sure the timing's right
- Perhaps recycle and test your assumptions again

Exercise

Take out your notes for your own writing assignment and answer the following questions. (You can't answer them for the case studies in the appendixes because that would be stretching the role play too far, so if you have no assignment, turn to the next chapter.)

1. Do I have a legitimate reason for writing? Will I get a reward or avoid a risk? (If you answer yes, go on to the next question. If you answer no, stop here and choose another assignment.)
2. Have I talked to enough of the right people so that I have a "feel" that the idea is feasible? (If you answer yes, go on; if you answer no, stop here and schedule the appropriate meetings or make the needed phone calls.)
3. Is the timing right? Is the organization in a relatively quiet period or does the idea solve a pressing problem or pursue an important opportunity? Are the people involved ready to listen, amenable to change? (If you answer no, stop here and schedule a time in the future to try again. Meanwhile, select another assignment.)

3

ANALYZING
THE AUDIENCE

Analyzing the audience will help you to:

- Identify the decision maker
- Address the decision maker's concerns
- Decide how much to say

It's no accident that the very first step you take before you write involves a hard look at your audience, the ultimate consumer of your document. Most proposals fail because they don't persuade the right people to take action, not because they have paragraphs that are too long or a minor lapse in usage. Answering some very specific questions (see the Audience Profile, exhibit 3-1) will help you meet the needs of the people who matter.

You will note that the last question in the profile is "Should I write or speak?" We will assume that you intend to write, since writing is the topic of this book. But if you have the choice, you will be in a better position to determine whether a written proposal or a spoken one is more likely to get the action you want after answering the first questions on the profile.

Exhibit 3-1.   Audience profile.

Who is the decision maker or primary reader?

What question did or might the decision maker ask?

How much credibility do I have with the decision maker?

How much does the decision maker know about the subject?

What is the decision maker's view of the subject?

What is the decision maker's managerial style?

Who will influence the decision maker? What do they know? How might they react?

What question do I want to answer?

What do I want the decision maker to do?

Should I write or speak?

Who Is the Decision Maker or Primary Reader?

Ask yourself: Who is going to take action on this proposal or information? That's the person (or people) to focus on. Everything you write will be aimed at meeting his or her needs.

If you immediately come up with the name of the decision maker, and he is someone you know, your job is infinitely easier. But for most major issues, you'll have several names, and some of them will be unknown quantities — your boss's boss, for example, or someone outside the organization. And often the ultimate decision maker (or makers) is not the person to whom the memo or report is addressed. In that case both the addressee and the people in the position to act are the decision makers.

What Question Did or Might the Decision Maker Ask?

It helps to consider every piece of writing as the answer to a question the reader has asked. If someone above you in the organization has asked you for a report or memo, it's possible you already know the question. Unfortunately, because many managers don't know how to give assignments, you may have been asked to "Give me a report on X" or "Write me a memo about the meeting." Neither of these is particularly helpful — in fact, they invite the writer to do endless research and then dump everything he or she knows on a piece of paper and send it along. If you get one of these marshmallow assignments, do a bit of delicate probing along the lines of "Could you tell me a bit more about what you're interested in?" Usually, people will respond to this since you're trying to save them time in the long run. There's always the occasional person, however, who believes it is a subordinate's obligation to read his mind. Keep asking questions, or — if all else fails — ask yourself, if I were in his position, what would I really want to know?

Remember, too, that managers have a bias in favor of taking action — undigested analysis and philosophical treatises leave them cold; so even if the assignment was "Tell me about the problems in the plant," the real question was probably more specific; for example, "What should we do about the absenteeism problem?"

If you think the reader only wants to know the problem, and not the answer, ask yourself whether you are avoiding sticking your neck out. Completed staff work, in military terms, means not only identifying the problem, but solving it.

If you are writing because you have an idea, you will have to plant the question (see chapter 6). For now, though, assume the question exists. Presumably it is either "Why should I do . . . ," or if the reader has already accepted your ideas, "How should I do . . . ." Management questions are almost always why or how questions.

If you're writing to inform subordinates of a decision already taken, you're answering a different question, namely, "How does this affect me?" It may be hard to conceive of your subordinates as decision makers, but to the extent that their wholehearted co-operation or indifference can affect the implementation of a decision, that's the way to view them.

Be sure you specify what it is the reader wants to know. "Why should I agree with your idea?" is vague. "Why should I spend $1 million to expand the galoshes factory in Farashes?" is specific. The more specifically you state the question, the more likely you will be to address the reader's concerns.

How Much Credibility Do I Have with the Decision Maker?

Credibility can come from many sources — your position in the organization, your experience at other companies, your technical expertise, your informal influence with key people, your knowledge of how things work in the organization, your likability — and it's different each time you write. It's important to determine how much credibility you have with the decision maker because your ability to persuade depends on three elements:

- The decision maker's willingness to hear the message
- The logic of your argument
- Your credibility

If you are the accepted expert on a subject and the reader will not question your authority, you sound insecure if you spend excessive time on detail. If you have little credibility and you don't develop support for your position, you'll shoot yourself in the foot. If you are telling the decision maker something he or she is eager to hear, you may not need to go into great detail.

If, however, the reader will find the message unpalatable, you may need to build some credibility for yourself by detailing your research or experience. The answer to this question will help you decide how much detail you must include and how much you must say about the work you did in coming to a conclusion.

How Much Does the Decision Maker Know about the Subject?

Knowing what the decision maker knows is essential to prevent befuddlement at lack of detail or irritation with excessive detail. If you're addressing a vice-president with an accounting background, you won't have to define FAS-5. On the other hand, if you are writing to a vice-president of marketing about an IRS regulation, you will have to explain technical terms. If you and your boss have been wrestling with a problem in the word-processing department for the past six months, you can skip the history of the problem. If you're a consultant writing an initial approach letter to the CEO of a privately held corporation, you won't start "As the CEO of a privately held corporation, you already know that . . ." and go on for three dense paragraphs about things that, indeed, he does already know. (One CEO sent us a similar letter he'd received, with the initial three paragraphs crossed out and "B.S." written in the margin next to each one — probably not the reaction the consultant was hoping for.) If you're writing to subordinates, they need to know enough about why you did something to be convinced that you know what you're doing and that they can trust you.

The answer to this question will lead you to include the right amount of information and to use appropriate language.

don't restate what is already [handwritten margin note]

What Is the Decision Maker's View of the Subject?

This is a vital question because it starts you along the road to understanding the criteria on which the decision maker will judge your communication. Does everything he says come with a dollar sign attached? Is she the "keeper of the flame" as far as the organizational culture is concerned? Does he worry a great deal about control issues because the outside accountants have said the company needs to tighten up? Does the phrase "quality products" have a very specific meaning to her? Is he under fire, simply wanting the complaints to stop? The more ideas you can jot down at this phase, the better.

get to know the decision maker personally then often

If you don't know the decision maker, first ask questions of someone who does — such questions aren't presumptuous, they're part of doing your job. If all else fails, you can speculate; a director of internal audit is concerned with a whole constellation of issues that are vastly different than those of a plant manager. The CEO hired to "clean house" will have different concerns than the CEO who's been in charge for twenty years and reaches retirement age next December. Try to make educated guesses rather than easy assumptions. The most usual assumption is "The decision maker cares about exactly the same things I do," and that assumption is *always* wrong.

What Is the Decision Maker's Managerial Style?

Management theorists have beaten style (as opposed to substance) issues to death, but it's worth thinking about how the people involved make decisions and how they like to deal with problems and people. You can get clues from observation: does the decision maker like to analyze data carefully — does his comfort level increase with stacks of technical back-up? Then you should follow all the rules for making a tight, logical argument and include all the data in an appendix. Does the decision maker seem to make decisions based on intuition? You still can't avoid all the preparation needed to make a logical argument, but you'll want to deliver your data with a creative approach, either by creating word images of what you want to do or by including visuals. Are you dealing with a get-to-the-point person or someone who wants the options laid out? Does the decision maker constantly want to "talk things out," or does she end conversations with "give me a memo on that." Answering these kinds of questions helps you meet the reader's needs.

Who Will Influence the Decision Maker? What Do They Know? How Might They React?

Even if they're not decision makers, people involved in the success of your proposal must be considered. You've already dealt with many of these power brokers in the course of establishing support for your ideas. Knowing what the people involved care about allows you to address their concerns in the proposal, speak with them, or write another memo. For example, if one of the people involved is the corporate director of public relations, you'll need to make sure you deal with any "image" considerations even though that's not at the top of the decision maker's list of criteria.

What Question Do I Want to Answer?

Often when you've been asked to do some troubleshooting, you find that the decision maker has been asking the wrong question. For example, he may have asked, "What should we do to reduce our head count?" After solving the problem, you decide the question you want to answer is broader: "What can we do to cut costs?" Getting the right question is vital because the body of the document is the answer to that question. When you write, remember that the question you've been asked is also important, because you'll have to alert the decision maker early on that you've changed the emphasis.

What Do I Want the Decision Maker to Do?

no action = don't write

You need to know what the next step is before you can close the deal. This question is also one of the tests of whether you should be writing at all. If you don't have any action in mind, don't write.

Should I Write or Speak?

write

The sheer ~~size~~ of many organizations dictates that most messages be written. When it's simply impractical to get people together for meetings or presentations, people stay informed and make decisions on the basis of memos and reports. Many large organizations also have a writing "culture." People are proud of excellence in written communication, and writing skill is a recognized criterion for advancement. Furthermore, in some organizations keeping permanent (which usually means written) records is vital both because American society is increasingly litigious and because accelerated employee turnover means that the organization's history cannot be safely left to long-time employees. But ~~issues fraught with controversy are best dealt with in person,~~ especially if the whole organization is in turmoil because of acquisition, merger, or economic slump. The best ~~written messages simply cannot convey confidence and trust~~ the same way seeing or hearing the speaker can.

Because writing implies formality, finality, and personal distance, it's a far less flexible tool than spoken communication — whether informal ("huddles" in the hall, meetings) or formal (management presentations). If you have the choice, write only when:

- The organization's culture demands it
- The audience needs time to understand and absorb the material
- The audience is large or geographically dispersed and all of its members need to receive the same message
- A permanent record is necessary
- The issue has been discussed to the extent that the memo or report is "surprise-free," and you have reasonable support for your position

Choose a meeting or presentation when:

- The topic is controversial
- The people involved must ask questions if they are to understand how the information applies to them
- Immediate action is necessary
- Participants can assemble easily

Don't consider the answers to the questions on the Audience Profile as engraved in stone. As you go along in the process, you may think of additions or deletions.

Ideally, you will answer all but the last three questions before going off to solve the problem. You cannot, of course, know the question you want to answer or the action you want until you have solved the problem. The answers to the earlier questions will, as you will see in the next chapter, influence your problem solving. Armed with a good understanding of who the decision maker is and how that person views the situation, you will be ready to establish criteria, which you will use in solving the problem and some of which will provide the framework for the body of your communication.

Exercise
Take out the materials for your own writing assignment or the case from the first appendix (you may wish to photocopy the case to make it easier to work with). Thoughtfully fill out the audience profile for your own situation or the case. The more work you do at this stage, the better — you'll refer back to this profile throughout the writing process. If you have to answer "don't know" at any point, write down how you might find out.

SUMMARY

To analyze your audience you should:

- Identify the decision maker who will take action on your report or memo
- Become familiar with the decision maker's concerns by asking:
  — What is the question the decision maker wants answered?
  — How much credibility do I have with the decision maker?
  — What does he already know about the subject and what are his previous views?
  — What is his personal managerial style and who or what influences his decisions?
- Decide how much to say by focusing on:
  — What questions you want to answer
  — What action you want taken

4

CRITERIA FOR SOLVING THE PROBLEM AND CONVEYING THE MESSAGE

Understanding criteria and using them appropriately is the key to being logical and persuasive. This chapter will show you how to:

- Establish useful criteria
- Use criteria to:
  — isolate a problem
  — evaluate and choose among alternative solutions
  — set the structure for your letter, memo, or report

"My people don't write clearly because they solve problems haphazardly." In our interviews with managers, comments like this cropped up repeatedly. To these men and women, proper problem solving meant analyzing a situation to find the parts or the cause of the problem, evaluating alternatives, and making realistic recommendations. Stating criteria to be sure that you leave out nothing important is challenging. If you master this technique, however, you will avoid wasting time on unnecessary research and will produce clear and coherent reports.

Quite literally, a criterion is a standard on which a judgment or a decision can be based. For example, if you are going out to look for a new car, you probably have some criteria that the car should meet. Unless you are very lucky, you won't find a car that meets all your criteria, so you will have to compromise and make trade-offs. The same concept applies in solving management problems. How do you know when something is wrong? Only by knowing the criteria for what is "right." How do you know which alternative is best? Only by knowing which best meets your criteria. How do you persuade people that the solution you recommend is the best? Only by showing them how it meets their criteria. (Most of the time as a manager you make a recommendation or evaluate options. If you are describing something, "criteria" equates with the parts of the whole. If you are telling someone how to do something, "criteria" equates with steps.) The value of thinking about solving a problem and communicating the answer using criteria will be quite clear as you work through the next two chapters.

Establishing Criteria

To be useful, criteria must be:

- Stated as assertions against which a situation or alternatives can be measured
- Based on the problem solver's, organization's, and decision maker's standards
- Limited in number

State Criteria as Assertions

Good criteria should be written down as complete sentences that include the words *should* or *must* and that use specific words. It's tempting to try to juggle vague criteria in your head, especially if you like to operate in the world of intuition or don't want to be pinned down to details. But only by disciplining yourself to write your criteria as complete sentences will you be sure they indicate your standard of measurement and the desired result. For example, when asked, "What are your criteria for your next job?" most people come up with a list that includes words or phrases like "adequate salary," "location," "opportunity for advancement," and "opportunity to use my skills." But these are not useful in evaluating options. To one person, for example, $25,000 might be an "adequate salary"; to another, the figure might be $250,000. Similarly, what location does the person prefer? Suburban or city? Sun Belt or East Coast? How fast does advancement have to be? What skills must be called upon in the job? Imprecise criteria usually reflect fuzzy or incomplete thinking and ultimately lead to poor problem solving and weak support for your recommendation. Good criteria indicate the result you want by including "should" or "must," and are stated specifically enough that you can measure how well an option meets that standard.

Look at these revised criteria. If you were the job seeker, it would be easy for you to choose among alternatives.

The position should pay a salary of at least $35,000.

The position should include benefits of at least $12,000, including stock options.

The position should be with an organization located in the San Francisco area.

The position should guarantee review for a major promotion after two years.

The position should enable me to use my analytical skills and strategic planning experience.

These are all precise enough to allow a choice among job offers. Not only that, they are all stated positively. Positively stated criteria are easier to work with than negatively stated criteria, and the arguments based on them are likely to be more persuasive. Consider this pair of criteria:

The marketing campaign should allow us to meet our plan goal for 1987.

The marketing campaign should prevent us from falling short of our 1987 plan goal.

Which one would you respond to? It's true that many people are risk-averse, but even they respond better to positive appeals.

Consider All Three Sources of Criteria

Criteria come from three sources: you, the problem solver; the organization; and the decision maker.

Your Criteria. As the person asked to solve a problem, you are expected to know, or to establish, the standards by which you will define the problem and select a solution. In addition to the criteria you set as the expert, you may also have personal criteria. Some of these, such as "The solution should help my division meet its goals," make sense for the organization. Others, such as "The solution should make me look like a hero," are best left unstated.

Organizational Criteria. The organization for which you work may have very specific criteria for making a decision, such as "Any property should provide a return on assets of X," or "Any project must exceed the hurdle rate of Y." If you're lucky, you're part of an organization in which people at the top articulate precise goals and objectives that can be used to develop standards for any decision. If the CEO has been quoted frequently as saying, "We want to produce the best widget in the world," you can count on quality being an element in the criteria you develop when you're looking for a solution to the production problem at the widget factory.

The Decision Maker's Criteria. When you are making a presentation to people high up in an organization, most of their criteria are usually based on what they believe will promote the success of the organization. (When you are presenting to people low in the organization, their concerns may be more personal.) But even senior managers have biases and preconceptions that may indicate to you some personal criteria or, at the least, which of the objective criteria for solving the problem are most important to them. Check the audience profile. How did you assess the decision maker's view of the situation? You probably wrote down items like "budgetary concerns," "feasibility," "state-of-the-art technology," "increased control," and "security of EDP operations." You may have jotted down issues of personal concern to the decision maker ("wants to make her mark on the organization") or pure biases ("hates consultants"). Anything you've written down should be examined carefully and, if possible, stated as a standard.

Exercise
  List your criteria, your organization's criteria, and the decision maker's criteria for the memo or report you are working on or the case you've chosen. Remember to use full sentences, including should *or* must, *and specific language.*

Group Criteria. Any time you are dealing with ideas, it is important to group like ideas together in a way that is meaningful. You will see, in the next chapter, that criteria give you a means of limiting the ideas you present to those that are crucial. (The only reasons that matter are reasons based on criteria.) At this point your task is to group your criteria so as to make them both more useful and fewer in number.

You probably noticed, earlier in the chapter, that the first two criteria the job applicant put down had something in common — they both related to total compensation.

The position should pay a salary of at least $35,000.

The position should include benefits of $12,000 including stock options.

By combining those criteria into one, the problem solver achieved greater flexibility:

The position should offer a total compensation package of $47,000.

After all, if the salary component is sufficiently large, the applicant can purchase benefits to compensate. Conversely, if benefits are vital, an impressive pension plan and health insurance may compensate for a less grandiose salary.

Why worry about limiting the number of criteria? Research has shown that although people can keep in their minds only five to seven separate pieces of information at a time, they can retain far *why* more information if the ideas are grouped as subsets of a higher-level concept. For example, think about how you deal with the tasks you have to do on any given day. Suppose you have a number of projects underway at the office plus a business lunch that will take you across town, as well as a few personal errands to do. To keep track of what you must do, you will most likely group tasks in terms of office, lunchtime (when it may be convenient to deal with an errand or two), and stops on the way home. If the office part of the list is long, you will probably group the tasks in terms of priorities.

Key Tasks
Write General Products proposal

Call Harry Blotz to follow up on May 14 meeting

Assemble budget figures for monthly report

Deferrable Tasks
Write letter to Jamie Tooms of Sullivan — thanks for setting up meeting

Review journals

Delegatable Tasks
Write Simson re lost proposal (Get Sally to draft)

Call Colins on phone charges (Sam)

Alternatively (and less usefully), you might group the list in terms of time slots, grouping together all the writing assignments if you plan to come into the office an hour early to get your writing done. Your secretary, however, whose mental filing system is different from yours, might group your "to do" list in terms of reports, phone calls, and projects. The message is clear; if you want your reader to understand the relationship you see among criteria and remember them, group them.

Exercise
Look at the list of criteria you wrote a few minutes ago. Are there some that can be put together either to make a meaningful category or simply because they overlap or are redundant?

Using Criteria to Isolate a Problem

To be sure you have properly identified any problem, you should analyze it by breaking it into its components. For simple problems, you can do this in your head; for most, however, writing your analysis down schematically will help you see components and relationships, insuring that you haven't forgotten anything important.

Two tested devices for isolating a problem are the analysis tree and the flow chart. An analysis tree allows you to subdivide components into their parts to find any trouble spots. A flow chart is a convenient way to determine faulty parts of processes.

You draw an analysis tree by writing the question on the left of a page and using branches to show the problem's structure. When you already have all the necessary information and are simply describing something, the analysis tree also provides the outline for your memo or report. This tool is particularly useful in deciding what to write and how to organize your information. In one case, the senior management of a corporation instituted an incentive program that required managers to meet with employees on a regular basis to discuss performance. Having determined that division supervisors were likely to view the new policy as an unreasonable drain on their time, the personnel director, charged with explaining the policy, drew the analysis tree shown in exhibit 4-1, basing his categories on the questions the supervisors might ask. Their questions, as you can see, were based on their criteria for evaluating the system's impact on them.

If you have a simple topic, drawing the tree is a way of grouping your ideas. To write, you need only decide on the order (described in chapter 5).

Analysis Trees for Complex Problems

If you are dealing with a complex issue, you'll use the analysis tree to determine the cause of the problem. Although such analysis trees cannot be translated directly into memos or reports, they provide the framework for your research and organization. To draw an analysis tree for a complex problem, begin at the left with the question you must answer to solve the problem, which may be different from the question the reader might ask. In one case, a candy manufacturer who wanted to know what to do about declining profits asked a consultant for help. The consultant, in an attempt to determine the cause of the decline, asked herself, "What are the criteria for maintaining high profits?" and decided they were "Fixed costs should not increase" and "Contribution should not decline." She then drew the analysis tree shown in exhibit 4-2. By asking questions about each component or criterion, she established the direction for her research and found the components of profits that were not producing the expected results. She then could look for the causes of the deviations, again, based on criteria, and ways to correct them.

Many consultants and high-level managers find that drawing analysis trees helps them narrow the scope of their research. Ap-

Exhibit 4-1. Simple analysis tree.

Question: What is the new incentive policy?

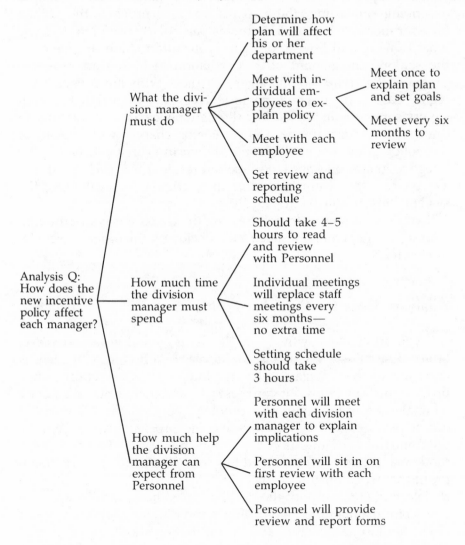

pendix 3 contains several problems, phrased as questions a reader might ask, and the analysis trees managers drew to analyze those problems. Testing your analyses against theirs will allow you to sharpen your skills at using this tool.

Exhibit 4-2. Analysis tree for complex problem.

Question: How can we stop declining profits in the candy division?

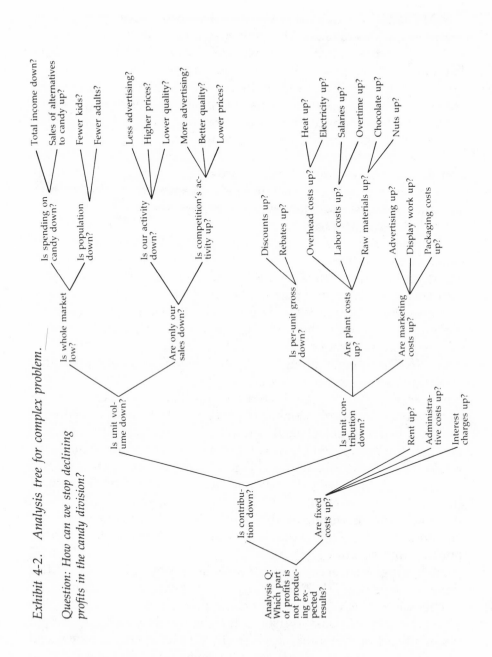

Flow Charts and Causal Chains

Flow charts are most useful in analyzing a process or the development of a situation. The new customer relations director of a major international airline, for instance, asked the head of Lost and Found to review operations in his department and recommend any necessary changes. The head of the department drew the flow chart shown in exhibit 4-3, which he used to develop a series of questions about how the department was functioning. Again, the tasks may be converted into criteria for a properly functioning process.

You can use a flow chart to analyze the development of a situation and to organize a chronologically ordered report. But flow charts as a problem-solving device are more often used to determine whether the apparent cause of a problem is the primary cause. Such charts are called "causal chains."

The principals of a law firm, finding that the corporation's net earnings were not keeping pace with its gross income, asked their accountant to find ways to cut costs. The accountant broke the company's expenses into parts and compared each part with county averages. Finding that total clerical costs, as a percentage of gross income, were among the highest in the area, although individual salaries were not above average, he concluded that the office was overstaffed. As a result of his study, several word-processor personnel and bookkeepers were replaced by part-time help. Within months, however, the lawyers found overtime costs had escalated and much of the work was poorly done. This time the accountant talked with staff members and determined that some were not working efficiently and that the part-time help was far more costly than full-time help. By changing some jobs and making several part-time positions into one full-time one, he cut costs and improved both the quality of the work and job satisfaction. Although he had correctly broken the whole into parts in the first study, he had not considered the components of salary expense or the environmental factors that affected individuals.

Such superficial acceptance of a cause is not uncommon. After hours or days of work, finding any cause is a great relief. One way to check whether you have found the primary cause is to develop a causal chain and ask yourself, "If I change this, will the desired result always or certainly happen?" Eliminating staff members will not cut expenses if the work cannot be completed by the remaining people.

Exhibit 4-3. Flow chart.

Receive Notice of Lost Bag	→ Complete Written Form	→ Put Information into Computer	→ Check with Appropriate Terminals	→ Locate Bag	→ Inform Traveler	→ Deliver Bag
	• Correct description	• Check information	• Call airports		• Call	• Check arrival terminal
	• Tag number	• Key obvious terminals	• Request specific checks		• Write	• Transfer to delivery agent
	• Contact number	• Wait 3 days	• Follow up for response in 2 days		• Give delivery time	• Follow up
	• Signature					

---

poor work   high total   low corporate
distribution → overstaffing →   salaries   →   earnings

                  intermediate   *intermediate*
primary cause   *cause*   *cause*   *effect*

Often you will want to use an analysis tree or flow chart to find the part of the whole that is malfunctioning and then use the causal chain to be sure that you have the primary cause.

Exercise

> *Think about a problem you are working on now. Divide it into its parts by building an analysis tree or by developing a flow chart. Once you know which component is not meeting expectations, build a causal chain. Following this process will increase your understanding of the problem.*

Armed with a solid understanding of the problem, you are prepared to solve it. Some helpful problem-solving and information-gathering tools are included in appendix 3.

Using Criteria to Evaluate Alternatives

If the problem is evident and you did not need to use criteria to isolate it, it is very tempting to get on with finding solutions — to "blue sky" for options and then come up with the reasons one is better than the others. Some people believe that setting criteria before they generate options inhibits their creativity. Coming up with alternatives before you establish criteria, however, may very well inhibit your objectivity. Once you have a "favorite" option you may become so enamored of it that you forget an important criterion. For example, a friend recently told us this story:

> Le Grand Restaurant sounded like a super place for an important business lunch I had scheduled. It serves my companion's favorite soufflé, the service is impeccable, it is quiet enough to carry on a serious conversation.

But I really did myself in; I forgot that Le Grand doesn't take credit cards and I had $2.50 in my wallet.

Since the major criterion was "must be able to pay with credit," the alternative chosen was a disaster. Establishing criteria first both saves time spent chasing weak alternatives and, according to organizational behavior expert J. Rohrbaugh, produces the best results when working as a group. He reports that groups that establish criteria first come up with solutions that are as good as those the most experienced member of the team arrives at alone. Groups that simply discuss alternatives and personal preferences tend to sink to the level of the least experienced member of the group.

Making criteria useful for evaluating options requires:

- Distinguishing negotiable from nonnegotiable criteria
- Weighting negotiable criteria

As we pointed out in the example about criteria for a new car, rarely do you find an alternative that meets all your criteria. Good problem solving requires trade-offs, and to make trade-offs effectively you must know what is most important to you.

Distinguish Negotiable from Nonnegotiable Criteria

Nonnegotiable criteria are those criteria that *must* be met. You can avoid wasting time studying options that will be unacceptable by determining early which of your criteria absolutely must be met. A word of caution: people tend to cast a great many negotiable criteria as nonnegotiable. To illustrate, "A project must not force us to exceed our budget" is rarely nonnegotiable (if your proposal will bring in infusions of money, management is often prepared to spend more than the amount budgeted). Similarly, "must be consistent with company policy" puts a straitjacket on many proposals even though "company policy" by definition is a codification of past criteria that may not be applicable under current conditions.

Technically speaking, "Any proposal must be feasible" is a nonnegotiable criterion. But since you would not propose anything that was not feasible from a technological or organizational point of view, unless your audience may question whether your proposal is do-able, you would use this criterion in your decision making but not in your writing. If you allow yourself more than one or two nonnegotiable criteria, you will severely restrict your options.

Weight Negotiable Criteria

priority

All the job applicant's criteria for a job cited earlier included the word *should*, which means they are all negotiable criteria, standards he or she would like met but aren't absolutely essential. ~~For negotiable criteria to be useful, you must know which are most important to you.~~ We use a scale of one to five to weight criteria because it allows distinctions but does not force very fine comparisons.

Let's look at the criteria listed by a staff person whose boss asked for a recommendation on where to relocate a key plant. The decision to move had already been made. In this case, the writer did not find any nonnegotiable criteria but did establish three negotiable criteria.

Negotiable Criteria

The site chosen should be the cheapest available.

The site chosen should have the best access to a skilled labor force.

The site chosen should provide the easiest access to our markets.

These are decent criteria, but if you ask "Don't you have any limit?" you would get a more useful first criterion. The last criterion needs work. What is "easy access"? Within a certain distance of major population centers (if the product is shipped by truck)? Close to a major airport? In the middle of a city? By asking these questions, the writer can either make the criterion more specific or generate subcriteria that will allow him to measure how each plant site stacks up to that standard. He might have revised these criteria this way.

Criteria	Weight	Reason
The plant should not cost more than $5 million $1 million for site $4 million for construction	2	Costs are less significant than location and labor

| The plant should be located within 12 hours of the major market, door to door | 5 | Our business is based on immediate availability of parts |
| We should have a pool of 8,000 skilled workers who can run our equipment | 3 | We need some to start but can train technical-school graduates |

Note that the writer was able to give a reason for the weight of each criterion. Writing down the reason for the weight encourages you to be objective. And you may choose to include the reasons in the memo or report itself.

Exercise
  Decide which of your criteria are negotiable and which are nonnegotiable. Check your criteria using the checklist below. Weight the negotiable criteria.

Checklist for Criteria

- Is each criterion written as a complete sentence? (Does it contain a verb?)
- Can the reader *measure* precisely how well an alternative meets the criterion? For example, "Any solution should increase ROI" is not a precise criterion. By how much? How soon?
- Have you grouped like criteria together and made a higher-level criterion that covers the entire grouping?
- Have you separated your criteria into nonnegotiable criteria (those that *must* be met) and negotiable criteria (those that are simply desirable)?
- Have you reduced the number of negotiable criteria to five or fewer?

Weigh Alternatives against Criteria

Unless it's a "go/no go" situation, you have some latitude in developing alternatives to solve a problem or capitalize on an opportunity. If someone has specified the alternatives, you are limited. However, if you were asked, "Should we go with the proposed program or scrap it entirely and try something else?" you can play with the "try something else" part to provide sensible alternatives. In this case, you may be able to modify the program in some way without losing your investment. If you're initiating the communication, you can be as creative as you like in generating alternatives, limited only by your nonnegotiable criteria.

After you have established criteria, spend the first part of your thinking-time just generating alternatives. Save the evaluation for later and don't reject any solution out of hand because it seems absurd. Devotion to the status quo can blind you to workable alternatives. Even some that seem ridiculous may be adapted to become workable or may lead to other ideas.

Be systematic about assessing the alternatives you've generated. Policy analysts have developed a quantitative technique for assessing alternatives that assigns each alternative a value (on a scale similar to the one used to weight criteria) and multiplies the value by the weight you give the criterion. Using this system, you can develop a picture of how well each alternative meets your criteria. The manager trying to decide on a location for the small-parts assembly plant did it this way:

Criteria	Weight	× Value	= Score	Reason for Value
		Location A		
Within 12 hours of major market	5	5	25	10 hours maximum distance
Pool of 8,000 skilled workers	3	5	15	10,000 potential workers ages 20–65

Cost less than $5 million	2	1	2	Most expensive location — $5.2 million
		TOTAL SCORE	42	

		Location B		
Within 12 hours of major market	5	1	5	15 hours from market
Pool of 8,000 skilled workers	3	3	9	7,000 potential workers
Cost less than $5 million	2	5	10	Least expensive location — below $7.5 million
		TOTAL SCORE	24	

This formal assessment provided the manager with a "score" for judging each alternative against the others. Using a structured alternative assessment allowed him to organize his thinking and save writing time.

Exercise
Using criteria, evaluate the alternatives for solving the problem for the memo you are working on.

Using Criteria to Set the Structure of Your Memo or Report

Criteria are the standards by which you decide which of several alternatives is the best or whether a proposal will achieve the desired goals. Since the only reasons for anything that matter are reasons that are based on criteria, criteria, usually turned into reasons, will become the topics for the sections of your report or memo. In the case of the plant site, the report will have three sections. One section will explain why the selected site is least costly or prove with data that it will cost less than $5 million; one will explain how the labor demands will be met; and one will show how you will reach your market in twelve hours. Having used criteria to solve your problem, you know your main point (the one thing you want the reader to remember) and how you will organize your information to support that point. You are well on your way to structuring your argument. In the next chapter you will learn the fine points of creating that structure.

SUMMARY

Thoughtful, organized problem solving leads to logical, well-supported arguments. Establishing and using criteria will make your task easier and quicker.

To be useful, criteria must be:

- Stated as assertions
- Based on the problem solver's, the organization's, and the decision maker's standards
- Limited in number

Criteria can be used to:

- Isolate a problem. By using analysis trees and flow charts to break problems into their components, the problem solver can better examine an issue.
- Evaluate alternatives. By distinguishing between negotiable and nonnegotiable criteria and then weighing negotiable criteria, the problem solver can more easily discern acceptable solutions.
- Set the structure for your letter, memo, or report.

BUILDING A LOGICAL STRUCTURE

Making a diagram that pictures the structure of your memo or report before you write the first draft is the key to saving time and ensuring that you meet the reader's needs. In this chapter you'll learn how to:

- Create an organization tree to show the structure of your memo or report
- Use the tree to check the logic of your supporting evidence or arguments
- Order the major supporting points sensibly
- Use the tree to write

Every effective management writer creates a structure to guide the reader through a memo or report — some do it subconsciously; some use the linear outline they were taught in eighth-grade English. We feel that the form we recommend — the organization tree (see exhibit 5-1) — is the most useful tool available for structuring a report or memo because it shows how ideas relate to each other.

Using an Organization Tree to Create the Structure

If you were introduced to the concept of outlining in grade school, your teacher encouraged you to think in terms of individual topics (a report on Brazil, for example, would include I. Introduction;

Exhibit 5-1.   Organization tree form.

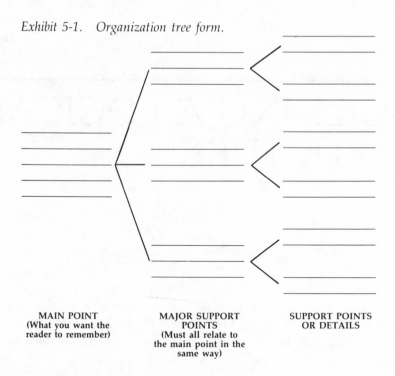

MAIN POINT (What you want the reader to remember)	MAJOR SUPPORT POINTS (Must all relate to the main point in the same way)	SUPPORT POINTS OR DETAILS

II. Geography; III. Political System; and so on until you reached the Conclusion). The tree, in contrast, forces you to consider relationships among ideas, to make assertions and support them — no phrases or topics are allowed. If you use a tree, you'll never find queries in the margins like "So what?" or "How does this relate to the problem at hand?" or "I don't understand why this is important to us." Furthermore, since the tree forces you to construct the body of the document (beginnings and endings follow different rules and are discussed in the next chapter), you'll be able to use the tree to determine what the reader needs to know to understand your message, and you will not recite a litany of problems while trying to decide what you want to say.

Using the tree also makes it less painful to change ideas and structure. Once you start writing, you're committed in some way to your phrasing (after all, you already wrote it down and you feel that you should be finished), and so you may let fuzzy thinking and phrasing remain rather than revise. It's much easier to see logic errors on a tree diagram than in a paragraph, and it's much less emotionally draining to correct them.

In addition, the tree is invaluable if you are involved in a team writing project. If you divvy up the assignments in the usual way, with each team member wandering off to research a topic and write about it, you're likely to find yourself up at 3 A.M. trying to glue unrelated pieces together. If you agree on the main branches of the tree first, however, you'll have a workable structure before anyone writes chapters.

Visual impact is increasingly important in modern management writing, and the tree helps here as well. A well-done tree lets you lift appropriate headings and subheadings directly from the branches and twigs. And, because you know what your supporting points are, you will limit your tables, charts, and graphs to those that support your assertions, saving the reader from trudging through pages of unnecessary data. (More on these topics in chapter 8.)

To create a tree, follow these steps. Be sure to use complete, declarative sentences because, as with criteria, only complete sentences permit you to check relationships and logic.

Start with the Main Point

On the far left of the tree, fill in the one concept you want the reader to remember — the **main point**. In most cases, the main point is your recommendation. (Remember the slogan "If you haven't come with a solution, you're part of the problem.")

You should be able to state the main point in one sentence. It is the answer to the question you want the reader to ask, and everything you write should support that point. If you feel you have more than one main point, you probably have more than one memo or report. Many writers try to do too much in one document because they feel that as long as they have the reader's attention they might as well bring up everything on their minds. This approach has parallels in personal relationships: the wife or husband who starts on one complaint, takes the opportunity to dredge up the time the recalcitrant spouse forgot his or her kid's birthday, and so on. Writing this way has the same effect on the reader that this kind of "trashcanning" has on the spouse — it causes tune-out.

Here's a main point that recommends a specific course of action: *Move the plant to New Jersey.*

What if your decision maker is unwilling to hear or won't agree with your main point, either because he has a preferred solution to the problem or because your recommendation doesn't meet a cherished criterion? Internal auditors frequently find themselves in this position. They may have to report that things are not good when everyone had been hoping for signs of a turnaround. And a writer may find, after working through an issue, that she flatly disagrees with the boss.

If you find yourself in this situation, talk to the decision maker before you write. Any major piece of writing should be surprise-free, particularly with regard to the major points. You may have overlooked an important criterion, and your recommendation won't stand a chance unless that's factored into the equation. At the least you can gain important insights from discussion.

If a conversation isn't possible (because the decision maker is inaccessible or you've got a deadline), you may want to make the main point your conclusion instead of a recommendation. In this case your main point will state the best course of action based on the criteria you believe are important. This strategy leaves the door open for those who have privileged information to disagree. Instead of the recommendation, "Move the plant to New Jersey," the main point would be: "Based on site costs, accessibility of skilled labor, and proximity to our major markets, the best location for the plant is New Jersey." Or if you must, "We should move to the location that best meets these criteria . . . ," thereby focusing on criteria.

Exercise
  Using a blank sheet of paper, on the left write the main point of the memo you are working on.

Fill in the Major Support Points

On the first branches of the tree write the **major support points**. For a memo or report that recommends a course of action, these will be *reasons based on the criteria* you established for an evaluation; for an evaluation of options, they will all be *criteria* or *alternatives;* for a description of a procedure or process, *steps;* for a progress report, *findings to date* or *parts of the whole.* All the major support points must relate to the main point in the same way.

Because the purpose of most management writing is to produce some action, we will use recommendations as examples in the first part of this chapter and explain how to use the same rules for building support in other types of reports and memos later.

Major support points for recommendations

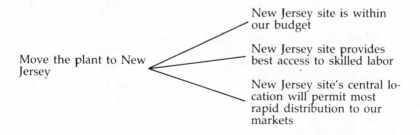

Move the plant to New Jersey

New Jersey site is within our budget

New Jersey site provides best access to skilled labor

New Jersey site's central location will permit most rapid distribution to our markets

Because this is a recommendation, each major support point must be a reason and each reason must be based on the way the alternative chosen met a major criterion. (Compare the criteria on the trade-off worksheet in chapter 4 with the major support points on this organization tree. A point like "Allegheny Van Lines has offered to move us next Thursday" wouldn't be included because it is not a reason based on one of the stated criteria.)

Your recommendation will usually not meet all the major negotiable criteria. Since positive arguments have the best chance of success, your major support points should still be reasons based on those of the criteria the recommendation does meet. You will, of course, have to deal with the downside somewhere, or you'll lose your credibility. Ideally, you'll have discussed the risks of your idea with the decision maker before you commit yourself to paper (and you would never propose anything that the decision maker would turn down flat because a major criterion was not met). If you can argue that the risk is minor, referring to it somewhere in the beginning will indicate your objectivity, and you'll retain a tight positive argument based on reasons.

Rephrasing is also possible. Suppose one of the criteria was "No proposal should involve layoffs," and your recommendation does suggest a minor reduction in the labor force. Your reason based on that criterion could be "This proposal involves only minimal layoffs." If an option does not meet a criterion at all, you will have to acknowledge that fact and explain why you do not believe meeting that criterion is critical.

If you've decided to hedge your bets by creating a main point that presents your conclusion rather than a direct recommendation, you'll still have major support that reflects how your preferred alternative meets the criteria:

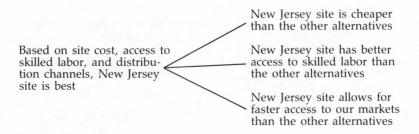

Based on site cost, access to skilled labor, and distribution channels, New Jersey site is best

- New Jersey site is cheaper than the other alternatives
- New Jersey site has better access to skilled labor than the other alternatives
- New Jersey site allows for faster access to our markets than the other alternatives

In support of these assertions, you will compare New Jersey with other options. This approach is more wordy and more tentative than a direct recommendation, but it does provide a lead to discussing all the alternatives, and some decision makers do insist on seeing all the alternatives.

Keep in mind that if you are actually evaluating options, you must deal with how each option matches each criterion. If the options appear as major support points, the criteria must be evident in the support for those points. If the criteria appear as major support points, the options must each be evaluated in terms of each criterion.

Inexperienced writers sometimes develop an argument like this in a feeble attempt to pass the buck back to the decision maker:

There are three alternatives
- New Jersey
- North Carolina
- Florida

Any memo or report based on this tree will take forever to make a point of any significance. The main point represents an "empty category"; there's no way of knowing why the writer selected these three sites out of all the possibilities. Is your main point really that there are three alternatives? Unlikely.

The most common variation of this anemic reasoning is the "pros and cons" argument:

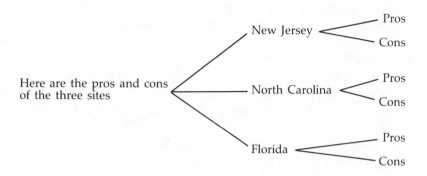

This writer is really dumping it in the reader's lap. Not only is there still an empty category rather than a statement of significance, but there are no criteria, no indication of importance, nothing but a list of "good stuff" and "bad stuff" with no way of comparing the alternatives in a disciplined fashion. People used to cling to this kind of lazy thinking on the theory that it made them look objective and thus more persuasive. But it has since been recognized that a strongly supported argument is far more convincing than a pro-and-con argument.

All the trees discussed so far have one feature in common: the support points all relate to the main point in the same way, and the main point makes a generalization about the discrete supporting statements. This is inductive support.

Support can be developed inductively (as we have so far), deductively, or causally. In management writing inductive support is the most widely used.

Inductive Support. Inductive arguments are most common for several very good reasons:

- Researchers have concluded that American managers think inductively most of the time. Since people more readily believe people who think as they do, using inductive arguments gives you a jump on anyone using a competing form of argument. Furthermore, the visual guidelines of modern management writing — bullet points and headings — are all conventionally coded by the reader as reflecting inductive reasoning. If you use them for other forms of argument, the reader becomes confused.

- Inductive reasoning is more creative and therefore more interesting than other kinds of reasoning. There's a certain elegance in working through a deductive or causal argument, but in many cases it's a somewhat sterile exercise, following as it does very set rules.
- Inductive reasoning is less risky. Because the other forms of argument all require chaining assertions in a set way, a reader who destroys the case for any part of the chain destroys the whole argument. However, if a reader disagrees with one of the supporting points for an inductive argument, he or she may still be persuaded on the basis of the other points, since all the assertions are independent.

To be valid, inductive arguments must follow these rules:

- The main point must generalize about all supporting points.
- Each supporting point must make the generalization more believable; they cannot repeat information or overlap.
- Any assertion must be supported by at least two points.

Although the sample tree in exhibit 5-1 has only three branches for major supporting points, your tree may have as many branches as you have truly major points (reasons, criteria, alternatives, steps, or parts of the analysis). Remember that readers can't keep in mind more than about seven ideas, though. If you have more than four or five points, go back and do some more grouping or consider eliminating less important ideas.

If you find that you have only one criterion (a rare occasion indeed), or if you are in the position of explaining why something happened, you may create a cause-effect argument.

Cause-Effect Arguments. Cause-effect arguments are usually based on the premise that if event *A* did not take place, event *B* would not happen. For example:

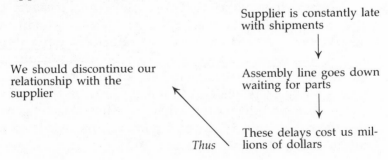

Here the recommendation is not supported by reasons. Instead, we're asked to agree that the supplier is the cause of our delays and lost income and if we cancel our contract, our troubles will be over. This assertion may be valid but only if it follows the rules for causal arguments.

- The first cause stated is the *ultimate* cause of the problem.
- All other possible causes have been eliminated.

Finding the Ultimate Cause. In the example above, you'd need to be positive that discontinuing the relationship with the shipper would save millions of dollars. You would do that by asking questions: Does the supplier get orders far enough in advance to deliver on time? Do the orders contain all the information needed? Ask yourself, "If I do *A*, will *B* necessarily happen? The key to knowing you have the ultimate cause is the word "necessarily." (See discussion of finding causes in chapter 4 for more on this topic.)

Eliminating All Other Possible Causes. Consider this causal argument:

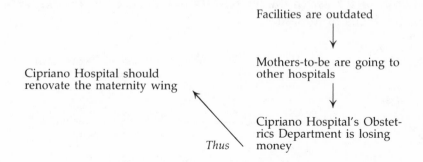

Are outdated facilities the only reason mothers-to-be are going elsewhere? Perhaps, since pregnant women generally go where their obstetricians are affiliated, too few doctors are affiliated with Cipriano Hospital. And a decline in the number of patients may not be the only cause of the financial drain; variable costs may be too high. In other words, outdated facilities may be a contributing cause but not the only cause of the dollar strain. If there are other possibilities, a disbelieving reader is likely to think of them. For that reason, it's hard to make a valid causal argument to support a recommendation if readers are likely to disagree. Here's the same recommendation, with inductive support:

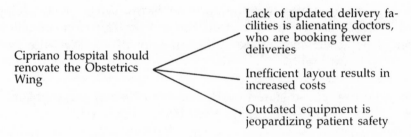

Cipriano Hospital should renovate the Obstetrics Wing
- Lack of updated delivery facilities is alienating doctors, who are booking fewer deliveries
- Inefficient layout results in increased costs
- Outdated equipment is jeopardizing patient safety

When there is more than one cause, an inductive argument is more effective.

A few additional words of advice:

Don't Confuse Correlation with Causality. Just because one event happens after another doesn't mean one is the cause and one is the effect. In the days when football was a fall sport, one humorist "proved" that football caused winter. After all, didn't winter always occur after the start of football season? When the season was over, didn't the weather soon warm up? And so on.

Look for a Flaw in the System Rather Than a Person to Blame. Consider this argument:

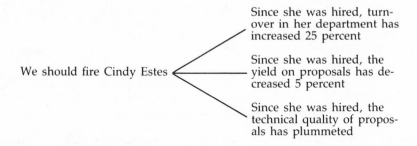

We should fire Cindy Estes
- Since she was hired, turnover in her department has increased 25 percent
- Since she was hired, the yield on proposals has decreased 5 percent
- Since she was hired, the technical quality of proposals has plummeted

If you are going to blame a person, you should be able to prove that the individual actually "caused" the problem.

The forms we've been discussing — inductive and cause effect — are the only forms that really work to support recommendations, except when the decision maker is *totally* unwilling to hear your message. The other forms of support — deductive and process of elimination (or *if/then*, which is developed the same way) — rely on a chain of logic to trap the reader into agreeing with the unpalatable conclusion or recommendation. We strongly believe that readers today are too savvy to wait patiently while the writer plays mind games. Most readers, in fact, when thwarted in their efforts to find out what the writer is getting at, will simply flip to the end of the memo or report (and throw a tantrum on finding the bad news there, without reading all your glorious support). In any case, relying on one of these other forms of argument generally means you've failed to analyze the political environment, the timing, or the reader's criteria. In essence, you've failed to do the preparation necessary to make an open, honest argument for your point of view.

However, if you believe that your only hope is to hold the bad news until the end, you may consider an alternative form of support.

Deductive Support. There are numerous forms of deductive argument. The following example is one of the most popular.

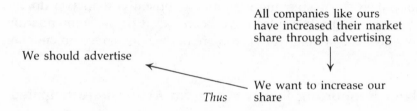

This argument has a major premise, which must be supported with evidence, of course, because the reader will not accept your simple statement that all companies like yours have increased share through advertising; a minor premise that repeats one part of the major premise; and a conclusion. The disadvantages of this form of argument are these: first, you'll need to spend endless pages proving the major premise and if the reader doesn't believe you, your argument is destroyed. Second, there's only one criterion here, "We must increase our share" (the concept on which the minor premise is based), and major decisions rarely depend on fulfilling only one criterion. It is true that if the reader does agree with your major premise and your minor premise, the conclusion is inescapable. But you should never underestimate a reader's ability to poke holes in this kind of argument.

Process-of-Elimination Arguments. Process-of-elimination arguments, intended to trap the reader, often trap the writer instead.

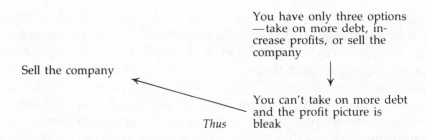

If there are truly only three options and if two have been foreclosed, the reader really must take the third option. But it's a very uncreative reader who can't find more options than the ones you suggest or, failing that, find reasons why the two options you've eliminated will, in fact, work. Furthermore, this kind of argument is especially tricky if you're writing internally (as opposed to relying on your superior knowledge as an outside consultant). It sounds very much as if you're telling the boss how to run the business, and the boss quite likely knows far more about the business than you do.

So far, all our examples have been based on recommendations. How does the system work if you are not making a recommendation?

Major Supporting Points When No Action Is Anticipated

You'll recall that when you filled out the audience profile, we suggested that if you didn't anticipate action, you should think hard about whether you should write it all. Here are some examples in which no action is anticipated.

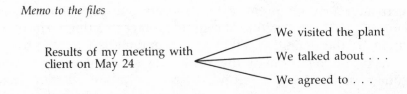

It's hard to believe that anyone, especially a reader in the future, grazing through the files, would be interested in the first two points. If your purpose is to jog your own memory so that you can follow up later, "We agreed to" is significant. Ask yourself, "What is truly important?" Those "truly important" pieces of the whole have something in common: they are all actions that must be taken to follow up.

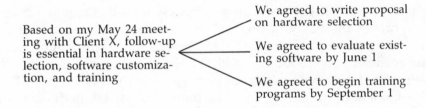

A memo written on the basis of this tree would help you remember what you're supposed to do, and if you were unavailable, someone else could pick up the slack.

If you're writing a procedure and no one needs to be convinced to follow it, you might as well use a flow chart, perhaps the same one you used to analyze the process, to guide your writing.

If you're writing a research project or an analysis (again, check the audience profile to make sure no action is anticipated), go back to your analysis tree and convert the analysis questions into statements (your answers to the questions). For example, based on the work outlined in exhibit 4-1, you might come up with this tree:

Remember always, however, that most readers prefer recommendations to conclusions. Conclusions only lead to another memo to answer the question "What should I do?" For example, a study of the effect of corrosion on the linings of pipes will usually result in some form of recommendation, such as "Use plastic linings in transfer pipes for the new plant," rather than a simple conclusion: "The effects of corrosion on linings varies."

Exercise
Write the major support branches for the tree you are developing. Make the support inductive if possible.

Develop Sufficient Further Support

To the right of each major support point branch, write statements that provide evidence or logical support for each of your major support points. These branches may be assertions that require further support, or they may in themselves provide adequate support so that you can stop. (The answer to the question "How much does the reader know about the subject?" in the audience profile will help you decide how much support you need.) This support, like the major support points, must be inductive, causal, deductive, or process-of-elimination and must follow the rules for whichever kind of support it is. For anything major, this means extending the twigs to the right much farther than shown on the form in exhibit 5-1. Taking the example we've been working with, let's expand on our support for the recommendation to relocate the plant.

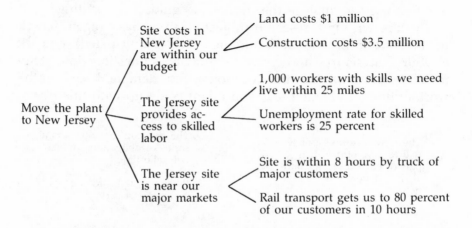

You'll notice that the first set of twigs refers back to the subcriteria we used to measure the total cost of the plant and that all support is built inductively. You'll also notice that there are at least two twigs for every piece of support. It you find yourself with only one twig, that means you're either restating the point to the left or you haven't provided enough evidence to support your assertion. All twigs attached to an assertion relate to that assertion in the same way. For the top branch, the twigs are reasons based on subcriteria. For the middle branch, one is the individual finding (showing actual numbers) that proves enough skilled workers exist; the other is a statement that at least 200 of these workers can be instantly available. The third branch is supported by two independent pieces of support.

Exercise
   Build support for each of your major point branches, continuing until you believe the reader, if told what you have written, would ask no further questions.

Check the Tree for Logic

Once you've created your tree, put it aside for a few hours and come back to it. When you pick it up again, examine it for logical flaws, using the following checklist and the rules of developing arguments.

CHECKLIST FOR ORGANIZATION TREE

- Is the main point the one concept you want the reader to remember? (This statement will be the recommendation or overriding generalization about the analysis.)
- Do the major support points all relate to the main point in the same way? (In a recommendation, these will all be reasons based on criteria; in an evaluation of alternatives, either alternatives or criteria; in an implementation plan, steps; in a progress report, the parts of the analysis.)
- Do the points to the right of any assertion all relate to that assertion in the same way?
- At each level of inference, does the statement generalize about the assertions to the right of it and about nothing else?

Here are some examples of common logical flaws:

The single twig

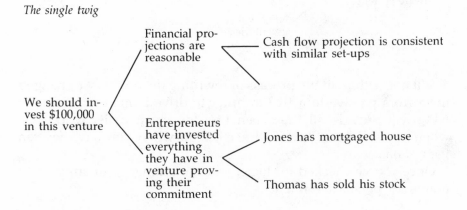

This tree, from a financial analyst's report to a venture capitalist, has an obvious problem. The tip-off is the single twig at the upper right. Sure, the cash flow projections are realistic, but what about other elements? What if interest rates take a leap? If you only have one support point, consider whether you've left something out.

Overlap
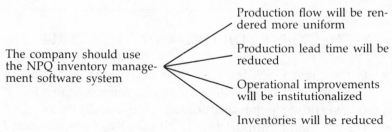

The clue here is the repeat of the word *production* in the top two branches, which may mean there's an overlap or an opportunity for further grouping.

In this case, there's a possibility of grouping the two upper branches under a still more general statement: "Production process will be rationalized," or "NPQ will rationalize the production process."

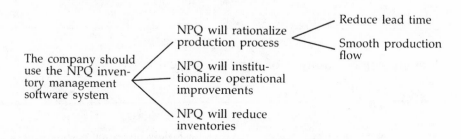

You'll notice that, in the process of rewriting the points, we changed them from passive to active in order to drive home the point that NPQ will provide all these benefits. It's much easier to do this when you're in the "treeing" stage than when you have written paragraphs.

Once you've checked for logic, you can arrange your supporting points for persuasive impact.

Order the Major Support Points

Ordering is relatively simple. For inductive arguments, you generally deal with the most important support point first, the second-most important, second, and so on. For a recommendation or evaluation based on criteria, simply check the ranking of your criteria on your criteria worksheet and, if nothing else came up as you worked on the tree, deal with the highest-ranking criterion first. If you and the decision maker disagree on which criterion is most important, start with that which is most important to the decision maker. The only exception, again, is if you've got a support point that is highly controversial or one in which your support is a bit shakier than in the others. In that case, you may choose to deal first with points on which acceptance is more likely before taking the tiger by the tail. For causal arguments, you start with the ultimate cause and work your way down the chain.

Exercise
   On your tree indicate the order in which you will make your points when you write the first draft.

Now that you've constructed a tree, revised it for logic, and ordered the main supporting points, you're ready to start writing by constructing a beginning. Beginnings are the topic of the next chapter, but before you move on, you should know how you will use the tree to write.

Using the Organization Tree as a Guide to Writing————————————

Your tree contains two of the three critical components of the beginning and all the important parts of the body of your memo or report. Using it to write is easy.

Any beginning includes your main point and the support for it. You might, for a simple memo, begin just that way. The body of your memo or report will have as many sections as you have major support point branches. Once you've written your beginning, you'll repeat the first major support point, either as a heading or a topic sentence in a paragraph and follow the discussion as far to the right as you've extended branches supporting that point. For a long report, you will have mini-beginnings to each section.

EXAMPLE

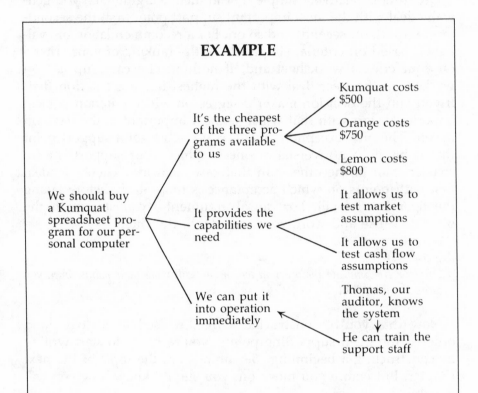

Memo

I recommend that we buy the Kumquat spreadsheet program for our personal computer network (main point). It is the least expensive software available for our system, it meets our software needs, and we can have it operating within hours (major Support Points).

Kumquat is the least expensive system available to us (major Support Point 1). At only $500 for three master disks and back-ups, Kumquat is substantially less expensive than either the Orange or the Lemon. The Orange will cost $750 for one master and back-up. The Lemon, which is available only with four master disks, which we do not need, sells for $800.

> *Kumquat provides the capabilities we want* (major Support Point 2). Kumquat allows us to test market assumptions, which neither of the other systems can do. It also allows us to test cash flow assumptions, which the Orange can test but the Lemon cannot.
>
> *We can have the program running within hours* (major Support Point 3). Our auditor, John Thomas, has worked with the software before to develop spreadsheets for several organizations like ours. He has assured me he can get the program going within hours and can teach the staff to use it by the end of the first day. (Note that this support is built causally rather than inductively.)

As you see, once the words are in place on the tree, turning the picture into a document will be easy. In the next chapter you'll start actually writing by developing a riveting beginning.

SUMMARY

Making a diagram that pictures the structure of your argument before you write enables you to build a logical structure that will save you time and will clarify your position to the reader.

To use an organization tree to create structure you should place:

- The main point on the left
- The major supporting points or branches to the right of the main point
- The further supporting points or twigs to the right of the branches

Major support points are

- Usually based on negotiable criteria
- Developed by
  — inductive support
  — cause-effect support
  — deductive support
  — process-of-elimination support

Inductive support must follow these rules:

- The main point must generalize about all supporting points
- Each supporting point must make a generalization more believable; they cannot repeat or overlap
- Any assertion must be supported by at least two points

Cause-effect support must follow these rules:

- The first cause stated is the ultimate cause of the problem
- All other possible causes have been eliminated

To check the tree for logic ask yourself the following questions:

- Is the main point the one concept you want the reader to remember?
- Do the major supporting points all relate to the main point in the same way?
- Do the points to the right of any assertion all relate to that assertion in the same way?
- At each level of inference, does the statement generalize about the assertions to the right of it and about nothing else?

To use the tree to write, remember:

- Any beginning includes your main point and the support for it
- The body of your report will have as many sections as you have major support branches

6

BEGINNINGS AND ENDINGS: WHAT, WHY, AND HOW

Most readers focus their attention on the beginning of a report or memo; if they don't find what they need there, they're likely to flip to the end. So beginnings and endings are crucially important. In this chapter you'll learn:

- How to write a beginning that will
  — compel your reader to continue reading
  — provide just enough information for the reader to understand your argument
  — establish rapport with your reader
- How to end your memo or report

Many writers are so afraid of beginning badly that they postpone beginning until the last possible moment and then ease into the task by loading on extraneous detail until they finally come to the point. Others charge ahead, making a bald statement of the recommendation or conclusion, piling up evidence, and then coming to an abrupt stop. The secret to writing good beginnings and endings is to focus on the needs of the reader and on what you want to happen as a result of the communication. You can ensure success by answering some specific questions.

Beginnings

Did you ever walk into a restaurant, look at the menu, and walk right out? Or, as we did once, taste the hors d'oeuvre and then ask for the bill? It's much easier for the reader to figuratively "walk out" on your memo than it was for us to walk out of a restaurant. Any beginning must capture the reader's interest and provide just enough information for the reader to understand and believe you.

Attracting the Reader's Attention

The beginning of a report or memo, like the beginning of a presentation, must grab the audience's attention. If you can't say something that fascinates the reader within the first few sentences, he or she is likely to set your communication aside or, worse, file it in the round file. To compel a reader to continue to read you must quickly let that reader know:

What the document is about

How you will develop your argument

Why the document is important

"Quickly" means within the first paragraph in a memo, and within the first page of a report.

What Is This Letter, Memo, or Report About? We have all had the experience of starting to read a letter or report and, several sentences into it, asking "What is this all about, anyway?" It is impossible to understand something if you don't know what it is about. **What** the document is about is easy to state — it is the *main point* on your organization tree.

How Will You Develop the Argument? Why should you tell an audience how you will develop the argument, thereby giving away your story line? Unlike the reader of a mystery story, managers and executives do not find the process of unraveling clues especially fascinating. The more a reader knows about where you are going, the more he or she is likely to understand your message. **How** you will develop the argument is the *major support point column* on your organization tree or, at the least, a generalization that suggests what will follow.

Why Is This Communication Important? Don't think about the subject's importance to *you* when you answer this question. Busy managers give their highest priority to material that directly relates to *them*, especially if it tells them how to take advantage of an opportunity or avoid a potential problem. Determining the most interesting way to tell the reader **why** is worth a few minutes of your time.

If you are asked to write a memo, it is reasonable to assume that the person making the request thinks the topic is important. In such cases the introduction might be something simple like this:

> You asked me (**why important**) to analyze the techniques used at the Perkins plant (**what**) to see if we could apply some of these methods to our operations. I have determined that we can adopt the following features (**how**):

Pointing out initially that you are responding to a request from the reader should guarantee that you have his or her attention. The word *analyze* presents a clue that the subject of your investigation will follow, and it does: "techniques used at the Perkins plant." The clause, "we can adopt the following features," lets the reader know that a list will follow. Since this analysis is in response to a direct request, the body of the memo will also explain why you included each item on the list.

While "you asked me" will usually get the reader's attention, you will come up with a more potent **why** statement by asking yourself, "Why did the reader ask me to analyze this situation? What is the problem or what is the opportunity?" For example, instead of the beginning we just discussed, you might write this:

> After five years, the Morganville Plant is still operating at a loss (**why important**), while the Perkins plant is operating at only 10 percent below original estimates. We can adopt a number of the techniques used at Perkins to lower our Morganville costs (**what**). Specifically, we can . . . (**how**).

When you are initiating the communication, the **why important** statement is vital. As we suggested in chapter 2, you'll probably have discussed the situation briefly with the recipient of the report or memo, either in the fact-finding or support-building stage. However, the issue is far more important to you than to the reader, who by now has other things on his mind. The **why important** statement, then, must create the question to which your *main point* is the answer.

This beginning is clearly inadequate, as well as dull:

> The purpose of this memo is to consider sales goals and projections for the department and for individual salesmen.

Although he or she probably has some passing interest in goals and projections, the reader, unless psychic, has no idea why reading this report is important. Something like this would be more useful:

> As part of the long-range planning process, we have used the corporation's economic forecasts to develop departmental and individual sales goals. We have compared these with our most recent sales projections and found that the goals are unrealistic.

The **why important** will be different for different audiences. An internal auditor will pay attention if you talk about lack of control, while an operations manager will respond to references to cutting costs. If you need help, look back at the audience profile for clues to the reader's interests.

If you think of the beginning as a story that builds to a climax, you may want to start with the **why important,** which states a significant problem or an opportunity, and lead into the **what,** the punch line, which, in turn leads to the body of the memo or report. For example,

> Earnings growth is threatened by the failure of Model K-22 to reach its sales potential (**why important**). A study of the needs of the markets in which the K-22 is sold indicates that the best opportunity is in the small-car field. We should concentrate our advertising efforts there (**what**) because . . . (**how**).

You may feel that the best way to reach your reader is to give the punch line first, especially if the reader is willing to hear the message.

> We should concentrate our efforts to sell Model K-22 in the small-car

market. The failure of the model to meet its sales potential is threatening our earnings growth.

Once the reader is interested and prepared to go on, your task is to make sure he has enough information to understand the thrust of your argument.

Providing Just Enough Information

A beginning should include only what the decision maker needs to know to understand the argument from your perspective, and no more. Anyone with young children knows that when the dinner table conversation is beyond their comprehension, most children will indicate their loss of interest by tuning out (or tossing the peas around). In the same way, a lecture on the geography of the Northeast will cause a child who asked, "When will we get to New York?" to gaze out the window and count beer cans by the side of the road.

Adults are no different. A busy manager is interested in answers to questions, not essays or diatribes. How much you should say and how you should say it will depend on the knowledge and interest of the decision maker, which you check by referring to the audience profile. If other readers need additional information to bring their knowledge up to that of the decision maker, send another memo, see them, or append whatever they need. Don't bore the decision maker.

Define Your Terms. Pay special attention to defining your terms, especially if the reader's responsibilities, experiences, educational background, or reading habits are significantly different from your own.

All industries and professions have their own jargon. You can become so accustomed to hearing, speaking, and writing a particular jargon that you forget that others do not understand it. The writer of a report to the town council fell into this trap when he wrote this sentence:

Changing the residential zoning ordinances of the township to include a provision for average-density cluster zoning seems possible from a legal point of view.

What is "average-density cluster zoning"? Do all members of the council understand this term? If there is any question that a reader will not fully understand an uncommon phrase or word you must use, explain it.

The decision maker should know the meaning of every word in the beginning. If the audience is broad, assume that its members, while intelligent, lack technical knowledge of the subject.

> Average-density cluster zoning, which would concentrate residential structures in small portions of a subdivision, would both preserve open spaces and control the town's population density.

Acronyms and abbreviations are dangerous. The full title of any bureau, board, commission, or similar organization should be spelled out the first time it is used (with the acronym or abbreviation following in parentheses) unless the audience for the report or memo could not possibly misunderstand:

> The Economic Forecast Group (EFG) model provides a useful means of projecting costs . . .

Indicate a Shift in Emphasis. Sometimes, when you've been asked to write, you find that your problem solving has led you to want to answer a question other than the one the reader asked. If that's the case, you should use your beginning to explain and justify your new approach. For example, the marketing director of a fast-food chain was asked by the president of the company to develop a marketing campaign for the southeastern part of the state modeled on a successful campaign the company had just completed in the western region. The marketing director was convinced that the real problem in the southeastern section was the public's reluctance to patronize stores in deteriorating neighborhoods. As a result, she wanted to change the question in the president's mind from "How can we best market the company in the southeast?" to the broader "What can we do about declining sales in the southeast?" Realizing that she couldn't ignore the original question or answer a new question without making the change in direction clear, the marketing director wrote this beginning:

> In reviewing the marketing strategy we recently used in the western region, I found that the campaign was most effective in areas where we have modern facilities and a middle-class population. In searching for similar communities in the southeast, I found only two. The vast

majority of our stores there are in decaying neighborhoods. Store-by-store sales in the southeast show that we are doing well in the two towns where demographics match those in the west, but that sales are declining rapidly everywhere else.

The beginning deals with the president's original question but leads him to ask the question the marketing director wants to answer, "What can we do about the declining sales?"

If you believe your audience will find your main point unacceptable, you may choose to change the focus of the memo. Instead of making the recommendation, you may want your reader to agree with your conclusion by looking at how the options meet important criteria. In that case, you may choose to begin this way:

> Your concern with choosing a location for a new plant that will be within twelve hours of our major markets, provide an adequate labor supply, and not exceed our budget led us to evaluate sites in New Jersey, California, and Florida. Each location meets some but not all our needs; the final choice will depend on how you weigh the various factors involved in the decision.

This beginning acknowledges the question (where should we put the new plant?), explains why the question is being changed (there is no clear-cut answer), and sets out the new question (how do you weigh the criteria?).

State the Criteria. If your memo is a recommendation or evaluation and if the criteria are likely to be accepted but have not been argued upon earlier, you might choose to set them out in the beginning.

If your reader has criteria you have chosen not to consider, you need to acknowledge that you have indeed considered and rejected them. People believe people who understand them. If you ignore a reader's criterion, she will either think you are stupid or mentally ask when are you going to consider what is important to her? Either way, she is not concentrating on what you have to say. Therefore, before you get into your argument, you will want to acknowledge that you understand the reader's position and explain why you did not focus on it. (And the reason had better be a good one.)

Avoid Background Sections. The usual "background" section is a direct descendant of the introduction you were taught to write in English Composition. Many writers, finding it difficult to get started, warm to the task by writing a lengthy background section, a mass of stultifying detail that bores and finally irritates readers.

If the decision maker needs to know something about the history of a problem in order to understand a part of your recommendation, provide that information in the body of the document. Check your organization tree to see if you can use the explanation as support for an assertion. In other words, tell your readers what they need to know when they need to know it. Information is more useful when readers know why they are getting it and can apply it instantly; when it arrives as a simple statement of fact in the beginning, its value is not always recognized. This beginning (part of which was cited earlier) includes information that would be much more useful as support for assertions in the body of the report:

> Changing the residential zoning ordinances of the township to include a provision for average-density cluster zoning seems possible from a legal point of view. The case law suggests that cluster zoning is a valid exercise of the police power under the state enabling legislation. It has been instituted in three townships, A, B, and C, and there have been no challenges. Although I do not believe cluster zoning is the panacea, from a planning point of view, that it was held to be ten years ago, it appears to be an appropriate tool to preserve open space and control the density of the population both from your point of view and from the town's.

The fact that no legal challenges have taken place in three towns is supporting evidence for the assertion that this form of zoning is legal, one of the major points in the report.

For most readers, seeing the word *background* is an invitation to skip to the next section. If you don't believe this, be honest with yourself about whether you read every word of background sections, even when you are not pressed for time. As a client of ours told his staff, many of whom insisted on including background sections in their memos to him, "I know the background of my products better than you do. So if I need to know something, don't put it in the background section. I won't read it."

Being Believable

Readers need to feel that you understand them and that you are worth listening to if they are going to believe what you have to say. Again, the audience profile will help you decide what and how much to say.

Establish Your Credibility. How much credibility do you have with the audience? (Refer to your audience profile.) If you are telling the reader something he or she is very willing to hear, you don't need to worry as much about your credibility as you do when you're the bearer of bad news. Remember, you and the reader think alike, and that should be enough. If the reader will not be happy with the message, be sure to acknowledge his or her position. If the reader doesn't know you well and you feel you need to state how much work you've done, be brief. Instead of a blow-by-blow description of your analysis, you can probably get away with a phrase like this: "Based on a review of twenty-seven competitors in thirteen countries . . . ." This short phrase lets the reader know you've done your homework but leaves out the details. If details are important, use them as support or put them in an attachment.

Consider Your Tone. The tone you adopt in the beginning depends on your working and personal relationship with the reader. If you asked a co-worker who is also a friend to read and evaluate one of your reports, you would probably feel offended if it came back with a note beginning, "Your report is returned herewith." Wouldn't you rather receive a note that begins, "I found your report most interesting"? Yet normally friendly people often freeze into formality when writing. On the other hand, if a communication is directed to superiors, informality is inappropriate. You would not begin a memo to your boss with "Joe, when I saw you at the bar last night I remembered . . . ." You can avoid errors in tone by keeping your relationship with the reader in mind as you write.

We've said a great deal about writing good beginnings because they are both extremely important and difficult to write. You notice, too, that we have called them "beginnings," not "introductions." The word *introduction* conjures up all kinds of old ideas, like background, for example, that you should avoid. Think of the beginning, instead, as a contract with the reader. You've told the reader **what** you will say, **why** it is important, **how** you will make your argument, and only what that reader needs to know to **understand** and **believe** you. (See the guidelines for writing a beginning given in exhibit 6-1.) The rest of the report or memo keeps that contract.

Exercise
   *Using the worksheet for developing a beginning (exhibit 6-1), write the beginning for the memo you are working on. Indicate the **what**, **why**, and **how**.*

Exhibit 6-1. Worksheet for developing a beginning.

What is the memo or report about? (The answer should be your recommendation or conclusion; the main point of your organization tree.)

Why is the document important to the audience? (This statement should describe what went wrong, what may go wrong, or what opportunity exists. It may help to ask yourself, "What will happen if my proposal is not accepted?")

How will you develop the argument? (List your major support points.)

What must the audience know to understand the argument? (Check your organization tree with the audience profile in mind. What else must the decision maker know to understand your argument? If other readers need additional information, consider providing that information in a separate communication.)

What will make the audience believe you? (This may be a statement of criteria or something about your credentials. Include only what is necessary.)

Endings

In *Alice's Adventures in Wonderland*, the King tells the White Rabbit, "Go on till you come to the end; then stop." To apply this advice to memos, avoid belaboring the point. In most reports or memos, the beginning provides a summary — it tells the reader the main point and the major support points. In a memo of two pages or fewer, the reader will be able to remember what was said in the beginning, and your ending should simply detail the action you want the reader to take or the next steps. A long memo or report, however, needs different treatment. Any ending, then, must set out the next steps. In a long memo or report you will also want to provide a sense of closure, and summarize — give the recommendation and major support points.

Setting Out the Next Steps

Since most management reports and memos are written to initiate some action, the most effective ending tells the reader exactly what to do next. A reader should not be left saying "O.K., I agree. . . . Now what?" This ending clearly sets out the required action.

> The success of our organization depends on putting into action the plans set out above and modifying them as the environment changes. Taking these steps presents a major challenge but one that can be met if the board appoints a committee composed of several members of senior management to oversee the program, review the timetable, and consider changes on a regular basis.

The best ending also creates an opportunity for direct communication between writer and reader and establishes a time for action:

> John and I will be guiding you through this installation. Nevertheless, it is important that you establish a good accounting system before we begin. We will be glad to meet with you Friday to begin planning for such a system.

Providing a Sense of Closure

Endings should never include new information. Cliff-hangers may titillate mystery buffs, but they make management readers uncomfortable and frustrated. Suppose you came to the end of a memo about an advertising premium campaign and read this:

> We estimate that the proposed campaign will be less than 30 percent effective. This estimation may be high when we consider that we are entering the low-consumption winter season.

What if the estimate is high? What is the significance of a 30 percent effectiveness rate? How about:

> We estimate that, in spite of its low dollar outlay, the proposed premium campaign will be less than 30 percent effective and does not compare, in terms of payback, with the free-sample campaign recommended last week.

The second example indicates the significance of the 30 percent effectiveness rate and suggests something that might take the place of the premium promotion. It gives a sense of finality to discussion of the promotion.

Summarizing

Short memos don't need summaries, especially if the recommendation or conclusion is visually highlighted by bullets or underlining at the beginning of the memo. (See chapter 8 for more on graphic design.) In fact, in a very short report, you insult a reader's intelligence by summarizing. In a long report, however, the ending should summarize your thinking on the subject — it should reinforce the major points you want the reader to remember. This is your last chance to get your message across.

The time you take to write a good ending is always well spent, for a good ending will leave the reader believing you are competent and your argument is valid.

Exercise
If the memo you are working on is short, it will not need a formal ending. Make a note of the next steps somewhere on the sheet with your organization tree and circle it in red so that you will remember when you write the first draft.

SUMMARY

A beginning should:

- Compel the reader to read on
- Provide enough information for the reader to understand your argument
- Establish rapport

To compel the reader to read on, every beginning should include:

- What the document is about
- How you will develop your argument
- Why the document is important

To provide enough information for the reader to understand your argument, the beginning should:

- Explain your problem
- Indicate any shift in emphasis
- Establish criteria

The writer establishes rapport with the reader in the beginning through:

- Establishing credibility
- Using an appropriate tone

Endings should provide a sense of completion and leave the reader with something to do.

The ending of a long report or memo should summarize the argument.

7

WRITING THE FIRST DRAFT

All your hard work on organization will now pay off in writing the first draft. This chapter will show you:

- How to pick the best writing format
- How to present a long report
- How to get started and keep writing
- How to check your first draft to be sure it meets the reader's needs

When asked how the book on his days as a power-broker was coming, Henry Kissinger commented: "Writing is hell. And it's a lonely enterprise." Kissinger had three researchers and four secretaries to help relieve his loneliness. Although you don't have a staff to help you write, the logical argument you developed in the first part of the book should make you feel less alone. Effective writing depends on high-quality content and imaginative packaging. Organizing has helped you gain control of your content. This chapter will suggest ways to present the argument attractively and persuasively.

Presentation, or packaging, includes the format, the words you use, stylistic devices, and any visuals you design to illustrate your main points. Properly used, these elements indicate your self-confidence, intelligence, and understanding of the reader's position. The place to begin is with the first draft.

Choosing a Format

Many large organizations have standard formats. Some stipulate the order in which sections appear. Some (not enough) give guidelines about length. Some even provide fat style manuals giving very detailed rules. The U.S. Army, for instance, gives a rule for handling paragraphs that cannot be concluded on the bottom of a page — "Do not divide a paragraph of three lines or less."

Standard formats often make things easier for the reader. People accustomed to reading reports that follow a standard format save time because they know where to look for specific kinds of information. Using a standard format saves the writer's time because relying on a familiar formula requires fewer decisions than devising an original design.

But using a standard format is more like painting by numbers than it is like painting the ceiling of the Sistine Chapel — creativity is sacrificed to ease. It's all too simple to fall back on statements like "We're supposed to do it this way" when, in fact, "this way" is nothing more than poor style reinforced by habit. If your organization has a standard format, don't stray from it unless you have a good reason. If no guidelines exist, however, you may be in a better position to tailor your memo or report to the needs of the reader and the content of the document.

If you are writing for a one-page-only reader (check your audience profile), you will want to get all the important information on that page by using a modified outline form, an executive summary, or both. If you are writing for someone who wants to read the concepts and let his or her staff review the data, you will probably write a brief report and collect all the supporting evidence in a separate section. If you are seeking to draw attention to a problem, you may want to depart from your usual format to emphasize the originality of your argument. Managers who receive stacks of memos every week may overlook important information if it looks just like all the unimportant information that arrives daily.

Given the leeway to choose your own format, then, you will select the one that best conveys the information in a way that is most useful and pleasing to the reader. If you are writing a memo, you may choose a modified outline or prose format. If you are writing a long report, you will need to decide on the placement and length of certain information and sections.

Modified Outline versus Prose Format

The modified outline format is becoming increasingly popular in business and government. It makes heavy use of bullets and dashes to indicate major points. Frequently, major points are written as full sentences, but transitions are kept to a minimum. A memo in this form is concise and requires less time to write than one in paragraph form. Consider the following example (which would be only one segment of an actual memo), and mentally compare it with the paragraph we might have written instead:

A memo in modified outline form:
- Permits the reader to:
  — quickly identify important points
  — see the relationship between points
- Requires the writer to:
  — eliminate nonessential information
  — order the information logically
  — leave out such stylistic niceties as similes and metaphors
  — leave out transitions

As you can see, the modified outline form provides a strong visual statement of your argument. For this reason, it is effective for writing reports and memos that emphasize a few important points or for organizing a long report in conjunction with an oral presentation. In the latter case, the outline form reinforces the major points the author wants remembered; complex material can be talked through; and the written document serves as a useful reference. Although the example given here is not written in full sentences, important or major points should often be in full-sentence form to avoid confusing a reader or permitting a speaker to lose track of the arguments for an oral presentation.

Several considerations may work against using the modified outline. The form suggests inductive reasoning; if your argument is of another form, bullets will not do. In addition, its abbreviated language is far from elegant. Stripping the memo of all examples, analogies, and detail may destroy a reader's incentive to keep going. And because the form does not allow amplification, the reader may fail to grasp some of the more subtle points. For this reason, the modified outline form should be used only when extended support for the argument is not necessary or may be put in an appendix. Using the modified outline form for an entire memo also lessens the impact of the bullets. Reading such a memo is just as dull as wading through page after page of unbroken print. You'll want to weigh the advantages and disadvantages before choosing the modified outline.

Exercise
Can you use the modified outline format in the memo you are writing now? Try it and see what you think.

Format for a Long Report

Reports are more formal documents than memos and may follow a conventional scheme. They are generally accompanied by a letter of transmittal (or memorandum, if the report is not for public use), which tells the recipient why the report is significant. A long report may include the following:

REPORT FORMAT

Title page
Gives name of organization, title of report, date, and name of writer or writers.

Executive summary
Provides an overview of the contents of the report. This should include a statement of the problem, the major criteria, the recommendation, and some supporting evidence.

Table of Contents (or Contents)
Gives the main divisions of the report and page numbers.

Recommendations
May precede or follow the body of the report.

Body
Includes an introduction, the findings or results of the research, and the conclusions. The introduction, in this case,
will be longer than for a short memo. It will probably include
some historical material, since the readership of a long report
is generally larger than that of a memo or short report, and
because a long report frequently serves as a reference over
a period of time. The introduction will often include a section
on criteria, and may include a list of assumptions on which
critical findings were based.

The findings may appear in abbreviated form, with the
bulk of the results in the appendixes, or they may be expanded
upon in detail in the text. Again, this depends on whether
the material demands extensive explanation and what approach the primary reader prefers. Sometimes conclusions
are put in the recommendation section, but most often they
are in the body of the document as the natural development
of the findings.

Glossary
Provides definitions of terms (primarily for technical reports).

Appendixes and Exhibits
Provide the detailed data that support the findings.

Reports differ, of course, depending on their purpose and the
position of the writer vis-à-vis the reader. If you are attempting to
create a format from scratch, looking at the reports and style manuals
of organizations similar to yours will help.

For your own sake, you should decide on a format before you
begin to write. Changing your mind part way through the first
draft is a waste of time.

Beginning to Write

We have all heard of novelists who write and rewrite an opening
sentence, never getting it quite perfect and never writing anything
more. The hardest part of writing is getting something — anything —
on paper. Unlike the novelist, however, you have a good deal of

the final document *already written*. Now, all the work you have done getting ready to write will pay off. The conclusion, recommendation, or thesis statement, already in sentence form and ready to use, is on the left branch of your organization tree. Each of the section headings is written as a major support point. You have stated the criteria accurately and have written down the reasons for each. Your supporting data are on the branches. For you, writing the first draft is nothing more than stringing together the parts you have already prepared. If you had writing anxiety before, you should not have it now. Managers who follow this method agree that writing, at this stage, is simple. Your job now is to get started — and keep yourself going.

Creating the Right Conditions

How you get going and keep going depends on who you are. But whoever you are, writing takes concentration, and it pays to establish an environment that will discourage distractions. Time and efficiency managers insist on the importance of setting aside a block of time in which to write. They maintain that trying to write during the small stretches of time you find between phone calls and walk-in conversations is wasteful; it takes too long to go back and reorganize your thoughts after each interruption.

A scientist-writer we know claims he does his best work while traveling. He tells a story about sitting for two hours on a plane parked at the end of a runway: "I got more writing done in those two hours than in a week in the office. No one bothered me." One executive vice-president gets his best writing done in his office from seven to nine in the morning when no one else is around. Even after the rest of the staff arrives, the momentum he has built up carries him through their interruptions. Many professional writers work all night, and so do some executives. Then there are those of us who work best when the office quiets down after five, and we can postpone going home to make dinner.

Creating a conducive mind-set is part of establishing the right environment. Some people write best after warming up. Zealous joggers don't just open the front door and start running. They get themselves ready with ten or fifteen minutes of stretching exercises and sit-ups and then walk for a quarter mile or so before they step up the pace. If you aren't fighting an impossible deadline, you may find that gradualism will help you relax and write with more energy. Try reading a short magazine article on an unrelated topic that interests you. Savor the way the author gets his or her points across in print. Surprisingly, this will often give you a creative approach to a thorny writing problem. Then write something short and satisfying — a letter congratulating a friend on a promotion, for example. This step is particularly important when you're writing a long report and won't get any rewards until the tedious job is over. The whole warming-up process should not take more than ten or fifteen minutes.

Whatever you do to get started, you will want to provide a mental sanctuary from intrusions. Think for a few minutes about where, when, and how you do your most productive work. If you can discover what kind of environment motivates you to start writing and keep going, you can strive to create a situation as close to it as possible.

Setting Manageable Goals

Once you've established a motivating environment, you need to set reasonable goals for yourself. These goals should be attainable but remote enough that you will not be able to put off working toward them. One report writer we know will not leave the office until he has completed the five pages of typescript he expects to write each day. If he is inspired to write more than five pages on one day, he still writes at least five pages the next. In this way he is able to finish a fifty-page report in two working weeks. We suggest that, whenever possible, you use the following process to set goals before you begin.

GUIDELINES FOR SETTING A WRITING SCHEDULE

1. Establish the final deadline for the report.
2. Set your personal deadline two days earlier (nothing goes as quickly as you think it will).
3. Allow time to have the report typed. Add a day for proofreading and corrections.
4. Set aside time for revising.
5. Divide the remaining time among problem solving, fact finding, organizing, and writing the first draft.
6. Set a timetable and stick to it.

Picking the Right Method

Whether you dictate the report, write it out in longhand, or type it is a matter of personal preference and the availability of equipment. Writing longhand is a slow process. Most people who use this method do so because it is easy to go back and make changes. Some executives tell us that writing in longhand helps them think and keeps them closer to the project. We suspect that a preference for this method is primarily a matter of habit.

Composing at the typewriter or computer terminal is an acquired skill, but there are reasons for learning to do it. If your handwriting is less than terrific, life will be much easier for your secretary when drafts are readable. Words and sentences look different in print; errors and lapses are easier to see. And once you get used to it, writing on a keyboard is much faster than writing longhand.

Any manager should also learn to dictate efficiently. The immense savings in time make it worthwhile. Most people write about ten words per minute; the usual dictation speed is sixty words per minute. In addition, the ability to dictate succinct messages will be more and more in demand as portable dictating machines become more sophisticated, stenographers become rarer, and computerized typing of spoken messages becomes more feasible.

Dictated copy has the potential advantage of sounding more natural than written copy because talking is more natural than writing. Of course, "talking it" may also result in irritating repetition of phrases like "you know" or "of course" and the use of slang. It's easy enough to eliminate these problems during revision, however. Remember that no one gets it right the first time.

Many managers don't dictate because they're embarrassed or uncomfortable about the process. Dictating effectively is a skill that can be acquired only through practice. If you're a novice at dictating, think small in the beginning. Start with a short letter on a familiar subject, move to memos, and ultimately graduate to sections of long reports. The following suggestions will help you dictate more efficiently:

GUIDELINES FOR DICTATING

1. Use your organization tree to guide you.
2. Before you start the first paragraph, indicate what kind of communication it is — a memo, a letter, a long report? A draft or final copy? About how long? What kind of paper?

3. Dictate capitalization, punctuation, paragraphing. Spell out names, words that sound like other words, and words that have more than one spelling.

4. When you are making comments to the typist (corrections or instructions), be certain they are not confused with your text. We have all seen embarrassing asides that appeared in the final copy.

5. If you dictate afterthoughts at the end of a tape, leave written instructions about their insertion in the text.

6. Read and correct everything you dictate. Remember, the author, not the secretary, is responsible for the final copy.

7. Don't be afraid to dictate draft copy for later revision. Most secretaries would rather type from a tape than decipher an illegibly written draft.

Guidelines for First Drafts

Although you should not feel constrained by rules when you are writing a first draft (the point is to get something on paper), it's obvious that a good first draft minimizes the need for revision. Following a few pointers developed with the reader in mind can help you write an effective first draft.

FIRST-DRAFT GUIDELINES

- Be natural.
- Set up the reader's expectations.
- Review and preview regularly.
- Construct your paragraphs intelligently.
- Don't make assertions unless you draw inferences from them.
- Don't skip steps.
- Elaborate on the unusual.
- Use examples and be specific.
- Stay with the tree.
- Keep writing.

Be Natural. Trying to write as if you were someone else (presumably someone more important, more educated, or more sophisticated) will lead to stilted sentences and a stiff, leaden tone. Your major decision is whether to use the first person singular, *I*, and the second person singular, *you*. We recommend that you use both whenever appropriate.

It is obviously appropriate to use the first and second person singular when you are writing to someone you know, as you usually are in a short memo. Going into convolutions (passive voice, use of impersonal *one*) to avoid it is not only silly but is also a barrier to clarity. For example, if you are dealing with quantities of data, some of which have already been partially digested by other groups (outside consultants, for instance), there are vast differences in meaning among:

> My analysis of the data shows . . .
> The consultants' analysis of the data shows . . . *and*
> Analysis of the data shows . . . *(Whose analysis are you talking about?)*

Even in a formal report, the passive is dull, and the third person, unless you are adept, sounds foolish:

> The author's *(referring to yourself)* analysis shows . . .

In some cases you may be able to use the first person plural, *we*, if the report will be signed by several individuals or an organizational group.

Set Up the Reader's Expectations. Readers find what they expect to find. Therefore, as in your beginning, sections and subsections should always indicate what you want the reader to look for. If you clearly are going to discuss personnel problems, the reader will not look for production issues. A reader who knows you are going to explain several problems will look for more than one and will make a mental note at each major point — an aid to remembering the argument. If the list is brief, the reader may find it gratifying to collect all the points you promise. You say, "You can improve your sales in four ways." As you cite the fourth method, the reader thinks, "Ah, now I have all four." But an unending line of "first," "second," and so forth can be numbing. Don't use the device wantonly.

Review and Preview. You should remind the reader of the direction of the argument. Not, however, by talking about topics — "This section contains a discussion of the problem and recommendations for immediate change" — but by indicating the substance of the discussion:

> Achieving Atlantic's major goals of increasing sales and cutting costs will require significant effort. The programs described in this section are designed to build on current strengths, focus on areas of potential improvement, and provide a system of periodic review.

Reminded that increasing sales and cutting costs are goals, the reader will now look for programs to accomplish those goals.

Construct Your Paragraphs Intelligently. A paragraph without structure is as meaningless to a reader as a document that has no organization. A paragraph should be a unit of thought. Readers expect all the thoughts in a paragraph to relate to one central issue or idea and their minds tend to idle or race furiously when they have to work to figure out what the main idea is. Can you follow the logic of this argument?

> Our competition, the original equipment manufacturers (OEMs), not only have the necessary resources to formulate entire service packages, they could adapt our machines to their systems. These large OEMs dominate the market. They set the pace. They will not buy our machine unless there is a strong demand from end users. The end users will not buy the machine from us because they believe it is not yet functional.

What is the central idea of this paragraph? Is the writer trying to support the assertion that our competition can adapt our machine to their system? Is he or she trying to prove that the OEMs dominate the market? That neither they nor the end users will buy our product? What is the relationship among the ideas? It is impossible to revise this paragraph without knowing the answers to these questions.

We recommend that you construct your paragraphs from the "top down," as you have done for the total memo or report. Managers skim. Additionally, a number of speed-reading courses teach students to read only first and last sentences of paragraphs. If you want to be certain you are understood, it is best to begin with the sentence that tells the reader what the rest of the paragraph is about. You should be able to take your topic sentences directly from your tree and fill in the rest of the paragraph with the data or evidence you have to support that statement.

You may wish, occasionally, to use a deductive order and put the topic sentence last, when it is necessary to follow the steps in order to understand the point. In such cases, the first sentence of the paragraph must still be an attention-getter in order to keep the reader with you:

> The American public now spends 10 percent of the GNP on medical care. Of that 10 percent, the greatest proportion goes toward maintaining patients with catastrophic illnesses (those that cost an individual over $5,000 in any given year). Catastrophic illnesses can only be paid for through major medical insurance. Therefore, this insurance is important for every member of our staff.

In a report on the insurance needs of employees, this first sentence will focus the reader's attention on the need for medical insurance, although the last sentence is the topic sentence.

We have no particular aversion to one-sentence paragraphs. Remember, however, that a one-sentence paragraph will emphasize the thought it expresses and thereby de-emphasize everything else on the page; make sure that the quality or importance of the thought warrants that treatment. Overusing one-sentence paragraphs, like overusing any other technique that emphasizes, will defeat your purpose.

Don't Make Assertions Without Drawing Inferences. The reader should not have to guess at your meaning. If there is any question that the reader might say "so what?" or "why?" you should indicate the inference you expect him or her to draw:

> Both our sailcloth suppliers have closed down for two weeks this August. As a result, we are falling behind in deliveries (**why important?**) and will not be able to meet our commitments for the Marblehead to Halifax race.

It is now clear to the reader, who is waiting for a sail, that he will be out of luck. It would have been even clearer had the writer said, "Therefore, we may not be able to make your new mainsail."

Don't Skip Steps. If you have ever put together a child's toy on Christmas Eve, you know what we mean. The writer of the instructions understood that in order to put part *A* together with part *B* it is necessary to bend the end of part *A* thirty degrees. But you, the reader, do not know this unless you are told. If your document requires that you explain steps or if the logic of your argument is dependent upon a series of events or thoughts, don't leave any out.

Elaborate on the Unusual. The compare/contrast technique helps keep the reader's interest. Why is your proposal different from so many others that come across the executive's desk? What is it about the solution that is especially applicable to this problem?

Use Examples and Be Specific. You can save paragraphs of vague description with one pointed example. If you've been asked to assess the quality of a new management-by-objectives program, for instance, one example showing that a particular manager's goals are unfocused and unmeasurable will do more to convince the CEO that there is a need for additional training than five pages of generalizations.

Although general statements are important (no one, remember, can tolerate a blow-by-blow description of every detail of a problem), specifics make them meaningful. In a monthly report that says, "The sales force had a productive month," adding "In March, our sixteen travelers made a total of 400 calls, resulting in 210 orders" makes the claim much more convincing.

Stay with the Tree. This does not mean you have to resist the urge to add an idea that occurs to you as you are writing. As we all know, writing is not a linear process. You must, however, first plug any new thought into your tree to make certain it fits. You have worked hard constructing a tight, logical argument. It would be foolish to lose your reader through the introduction of extraneous thoughts. If you find you don't like the tree, by all means change it. But don't put it in the desk and forget it.

Keep Writing. This is most important. If you can't think of just the right word, put down another one and keep going. Or leave a blank to fill in later. If you have an idea to add to a section a few pages back, make a note in the margin and keep writing. If you stop to go back to rewrite in the first draft, you may lose your train of thought. Always keep writing until you've met your quota of pages for the day.

Exercise
> *Write the first draft of the memo you are working on. Look especially for thesis sentences, and previewing and reviewing. List the guidelines you failed to follow, and read the list before you start to write next time.*

SUMMARY

Before you start to write you must decide:

- Whether to use a modified outline or paragraph format
- What sections to include in a long report and their order

Writing an effective first draft requires that you:

- Choose an environment that encourages you to write
- Set goals based on the available time and stick to them

Keeping the needs of the reader in mind as you write will minimize your need to rewrite:

- Whenever possible, use the first person singular
- Set up and meet expectations
- Tell the reader what you have just said and what you will say next
- Be sure paragraphs are well constructed around one main idea, which is the first or the last sentence
- Indicate the inference you expect the reader to draw from each assertion
- Don't skip steps
- Elaborate on the unusual
- Use examples and be specific
- Write from your tree
- Keep writing

8

DESIGN
FOR EMPHASIS

Designing your memo or report to emphasize your points and constructing visuals that support your arguments are important packaging techniques. This chapter will help you:

- Find the most compelling format for your memo or report through sensible use of:
  — bullets
  — headings
  — appropriate typeface
- Construct effective exhibits that
  — emphasize conclusions
  — present complex data efficiently

Designing the Report or Memo

Readability and attractive design are essential to the acceptance of your ideas. If you'd like to test that assertion, empty your in-box onto your desk and see which items you choose to read. Chances are, they're the ones that are easy to deal with and inviting. Stylistic devices such as bullets, headings, white space, and appropriate typeface can make the difference between having your ideas accepted and having your memo or report left to gather dust in the "when I get to it" pile. Graphic devices can be used to:

- Focus the reader's attention
- Emphasize the logical development of the argument
- Improve readability

Bullets Focus the Reader's Attention

Setting your major points off from the body of the text underscores their importance. Compare the following conclusions:

To achieve your goal, we recommend that you allocate $100,000 in order to identify alternatives to coffee rapidly and develop selected products.

To achieve your goal, you should allocate $100,000 to:
- Identify alternatives
- Develop selected products

In reality, it is the centering of the text, with plenty of white space, that pulls the reader's eyes to the points, not the bullets. But most frequently writers use some device, such as bullets or dashes, when they list concepts.

Lists of any kind should follow certain rules if they are to be effective:

- Items must be parallel in thought and form
- Items should be in logical order

Keep Items Parallel in Thought and Form. Readers expect a list to be composed of discrete items of the same kind. For this reason, bullets can be effective for enumerating examples, reasons, criteria, and so forth but are not effective if the relationship is causal. Going back to our examples in chapter 5, you might write:

Kumquat is the least expensive software available to us:
- Kumquat costs $500
- Orange costs $750
- Lemon costs $800

You would not, however, want to write:

We should discontinue our relationship with supplier X:
- He is constantly late with shipments
- The assembly line goes down waiting for parts
- Delays cost millions of dollars

Although these are all understandable events, the causal relationship is obscured.

Also, because readers expect lists to "sound" the same way, lists that are not parallel in form are jarring. This example is parallel in form.

We should move to New Jersey. The site there:
- Gives us best access to our major markets
- Provides an adequate labor pool
- Is within our budget

Each item in the list begins with a verb. In the following example, the difference in form makes the points harder to follow.

We should move to New Jersey:
- Closest to our major markets
- Will provide an adequate labor pool
- Budgetary constraints will be met

Use Bullets to Suggest a Logical Order. If you have gone to the trouble of creating a list, the reader assumes you have also selected the order for some reason. He or she will assume that a series of steps are listed sequentially and that any other list is ordered hierarchically, starting with the most important item. Violating this convention will obscure your meaning.

Why bullets or dashes instead of numbers? Because numbers cause readers to stop and try to enumerate the ideas that preceded. As a rule it is best to exclude anything that might distract the reader.

Headings Show the Logical Development of the Argument

The reader should be able to skim the headings and understand exactly how you will develop your argument. Unlike a fiction writer, a management writer shouldn't expect (or want) every golden word to be read. If a reader agrees with the statement in the heading and moves on to the next section without reading further, everyone saves time. One of the beauties of the tree, as you saw in chapter 5, is that you can lift your headings directly from it with the major support points as your principal section headings and minor support points as lower level headings. To be useful, headings should:

- Be understandable without reference to the text
- Be parallel in structure
- Follow a consistent format

Headings Should Stand Alone. Each heading should be understandable without reference to the text, so that a reader skimming the memo or report can be carried along by the headings. Consider the difference, for example, between these headings for a report on the use of poisons in fertilizers.

Long-range considerations

Long-range plans must eliminate toxicity

In the first, the reader knows what to find in the section; in the second, he or she knows what you want to have happen. To be useful then, every heading should contain a verb from which the reader can deduce the direction of the discussion. (As when you write anything, active verbs provide better signals than passive verbs or forms of the verb *to be*.)

Headings Should Be Parallel. Because headings, like bulleted support points, are essentially a list, they should be parallel in form. You can test your headings for parallelism by reading through them without reading the intervening text.

Headings Should Follow a Consistent Format. The location on a page and the type size of headings indicate the importance of the subject to the reader. A misplaced heading sends the reader an incorrect message. Inconsistencies indicate that the writer does not pay sufficient attention to detail. To avoid any confusion, you can make your own style sheet, indicating the way you want to set headings. You and your secretary will then have a reference, and you will avoid switching styles halfway through a report. For a very long report, you may choose to indicate the level of heading by a circled A, B, or C in the margin next to each head. The typist can then refer to a key on the style sheet. This system is especially valuable if you use a word-processing pool. The format that follows is widely used for long reports in both industry and government.

REPORT FORMAT

CHAPTER TITLES

Chapter titles are set in all caps and centered on the page.

Section Headings

Section headings are also centered. They are uppercase and lowercase and underlined. If your argument is logical, you should have at least two heads at every level of subdivision.

Section Subheadings

Underlined subheadings, flush left, head each subdivision.

- If you are going to divide a subsection further, you may do so by using bullets or some similar mark of distinction. These sections should be indented.

  — This level of subdivision should be further indented. It probably would not be used in a report written in paragraph form. If you are down to this level of division, think about whether the point is really significant.

In a report that does not have chapters, you may begin with centered, underlined headings (the second level above). In a memo or short report, this level, too, is usually eliminated. A memo of three pages or fewer usually begins with upper- and lowercase flush-left headings because a short memo rarely includes so much detail that it will need more than two levels of generalization (subheads and bullets).

Since chapter titles and section headings are broad in nature, there should be some explanatory or introductory text between each of these and the next level of subdivision. The text should provide an overview of the major topic to be considered in the section, suggest what is to follow, and define any difficult or controversial terms. In the example about relocating the small-parts plant, a section might begin this way:

Location C Minimizes Capital Expenditures

Construction costs constitute 50 percent of the cost of moving our small-parts assembly. In several of the potential sites, the costs of construction are lower than the $2 million estimated at Location C. However, the availability of industrial development bonds and municipal power must be considered in calculating actual capital expenditures.

Municipality Will Issue Industrial Development Bonds
Mayor Whiffen assures us the municipal government will issue bonds . . .

With the availability of boldface and multiple typefaces on word-processing software, the visual appearance of documents is taking on greater importance. One interesting format is based on the premise that when people skim their eyes take in only about forty characters at a time. Headings are set in a wide left margin, with the text to the right, like this:

The $50,000 requested will allow us to:
- Increase our understanding of current markets
- Determine areas of opportunity

Increase our market knowledge   We can establish a data base on key markets that will permit us to update information as we need it for planning purposes. Data will be available in . . .

| **Determine areas of opportunity** | Health care and educational institutions have been identified as potential marketing opportunities but we do not have enough data to develop . . . |

Type Style and Size Affect Readability

In the old days you bought a typewriter with either pica or elite type and that was the end of it. Then along came typewriters with changeable "balls," and you had options. Now some computer programs can produce a mind-boggling range of typefaces and type sizes with a flick of a mouse's tail, and you have all kinds of decisions to make. A few guidelines and common sense will help.

- Limit yourself to one typeface for most documents. You may use boldface, occasional italics, and a larger size for headings. But changing typeface in the text looks like a bid for attention — leave it for the ad agencies.
- Use italics rarely. Italic type is harder to read than Roman type.
- Don't set large blocks of type in capitals. In general, capitals are harder to read than lowercase type. One explanation we have heard is that people don't look at whole letters when they read, but only at the top half. It is reportedly more difficult to distinguish among capital letters than among lowercase letters. Also, readers recognize words most readily in the form they see most often — lowercase. And some people view all capitals as a message from Madison Avenue, which they don't appreciate.
- Use clean rather than ornate type; use serif rather than sans serif type. (This book is in serif type — letters have little edges.) Serifs help readers distinguish quickly between similar letters — *g* and *q* for instance.
- Use a type size that is at least as large as standard typewriter pica. The point size will vary with typeface, so you'll have to experiment if your word processor offers options.

Exercise
Review the first draft of your memo. Add headings; use bullets where appropriate.

Constructing Exhibits — Tables and Charts———

Exhibits improve most reports because, to quote a cliché, "a picture is worth a thousand words." Well-constructed charts and tables help both the writer and the reader because they:

- Present complex material efficiently
- Dramatize major points
- Emphasize relationships

A word of advice to beginners: you can save yourself time and effort by examining the resources available to you. Your corporation may have a design department that will assist on important communications. If you work for a large organization, check with the data-processing department. If computer programs that generate graphs and flow charts are available, you may be able to save time and increase accuracy by having some exhibits made this way. You can also create professional-looking exhibits through the multitude of graphic software packages that are available for personal computers. If all else fails, materials from a local art supply store and a copying machine that can enlarge and reduce will suffice.

Whether you construct your own exhibits or have help, however, you are responsible for the finished product. If someone is working with you, make sure you give that person a rough copy of what you want and proofread carefully. Errors in exhibits are twice as glaring as errors in text.

Exhibits Present Complex Information Efficiently

Always present data in tabular or graphic form if it will save your reader time. How often have you received a report with a section of text that looked like this?

We noted a backlog of scheduled maintenance. Records indicate that:

- More than 20% of the relays are past due for scheduled maintenance/inspections. Approximately 85 or 5% are two years or longer past due and 1% are more than ten years past due.
- Over 40% of our transformers are past due for scheduled maintenance/inspections. Approximately 128 or 20% are two years or longer overdue and 5% are more than ten years past due.
- Greater than 50% of our circuit breakers are past due for scheduled

maintenance/inspections, 30% are two years past due, and 8% are indicated to be over ten years past due.

- More than 25% of batteries are past due for scheduled mainte-nance/inspections, more than 10% are two years overdue, and 3% are more than ten years overdue.

How long did it take you to read that paragraph? Or did you just give up and skip it? Since most people find a table or chart easier to understand and more convincing than a paragraph littered with numbers, the writer should have presented the same information as a table (see exhibit 8-1) or as a chart (see exhibit 8-2).

Exhibit 8-1.   A table makes data easier to comprehend.

Backlog of Scheduled Maintenance Is Too High

Type of Equipment	Total % past due	% 2 years past due	% 10 or more years past due
Relays	20	5	1
Transformers	40	20	5
Circuit breakers	50	30	8
Batteries	25	10	3

Exhibit 8-2.   Like tables, charts make data easier to understand. Charts focus on relationships, however, rather than numbers.

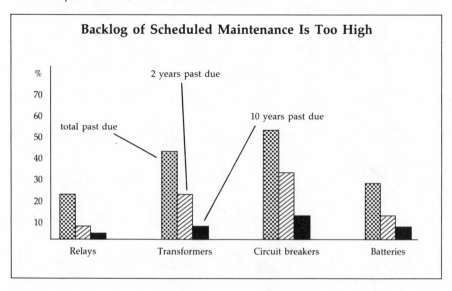

Making points visually lends impact to the simplest ideas. For example, think about this statement.

Earnings, which have doubled in the last five years, exceeded $1.2 million in 1986.

You know this is good news. But consider the greater impact of exhibit 8-3.

Exhibit 8-3.   Graphically showing data makes a greater impact on the reader than simply stating the numbers can.

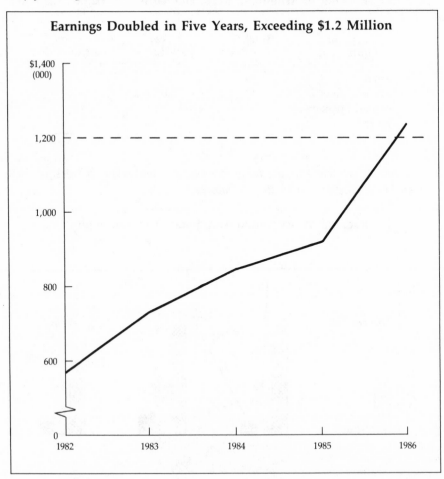

Effective Exhibits Make Their Point Easily and Emphatically

Each exhibit should be self-contained but tied to the text. A reader should be able to look at an exhibit and understand its contents and significance without reading the text. Many executives flip through a report looking at exhibits, just as we first flip through an illustrated magazine looking at cartoons. A chart should capture the reader's attention and transmit a message. If its heading indicates its significance and if all of its parts are clearly labeled, the chart is self-explanatory. When you can, integrate tables and charts into the text of a long report, locating them as close to the place they are mentioned as possible; exhibits are generally appended to memos. Regardless of where you put exhibits, however, you must refer to every chart or table in the memo or report itself and, in order not to distract the reader, make your point in the text. Do not force a reader to stop reading and look at the exhibit. It is far better to say, "Over 45 percent of our budget for fiscal year 1980 went for salaries, as indicated in exhibit 2," than "See exhibit 2 for budget figures." If you do not need a chart to amplify a point in the text, you should grit your teeth and forget the chart.

Exhibits in a memo or report are different from advertising graphics. Knowing what constitutes good design helps, but your eye is your best critic. The rule of thumb is to keep it simple; exhibits should be easy to understand, easy to read, and accurate.

Convey One Point Only in an Exhibit. To be certain that your reader will understand your exhibit readily, you should limit the data to what is needed to make one point. The first thing good graphic designers try to determine when a manager gives them a rough chart is whether the writer is trying to tell more than one story. Frequently, their first step is to break such charts in two. If you have several things to compare (the performance of four or five divisions, for example), consider using a series of charts with a combined chart at the end.

Exhibits can be more complex than presentation visuals (flipcharts, transparencies, and slides) because the reader can view the exhibit at his or her own pace rather than at the presenter's pace. However, the more you put on a chart, the greater the potential for confusing and distracting the reader from the logic of your argument. For example, the message the writer intended to convey in exhibit 8-4 is that sales and earnings both took a sudden dive in 1985.

Exhibit 8-4. Including extraneous information in an exhibit, as the dividend data here is, detracts from the effectiveness of the exhibit.

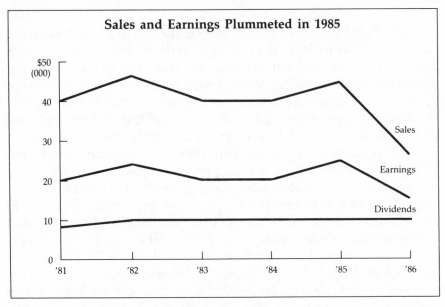

Adding dividends to the chart might cause the reader to consider why the dividend was not cut or how closely earnings approximated payout. Either way the writer has lost that reader.

Select the Most Appropriate Chart Form. Whether to use a table or a particular chart form depends on the material you are presenting and the point you want to make.

Tables consolidate quantitative data in a small space without losing any of the numbers themselves (as happens, for example, when you plot points on a graph). Although a table implies relationships, particularly growth or decline, it doesn't show those relationships visually. Therefore, tables are easier to misinterpret than charts. Note that the table below is effective in delivering its message because the relationship is fairly obvious — and it is reiterated in the heading. If attendance had grown in some parks and declined in others, a reader would have found it far more difficult to grasp the point.

	1975	1976	1977	1978	1979
Attendance in All Parks Has Grown over Five Years (in thousands)					
Allington Park	25	27	32	36	40
Pond Park	12	15	19	21	24
Freehold Pond Park	52	58	62	70	73
Samson Field	6	8	10	11	14
Center Field	12	18	22	23	26

Charts show sophisticated relationships better than tables do. Since more than one kind of chart can indicate the same kind of relationship, you should choose the form that makes your point most effectively. The following guide and the illustrations on the next few pages may help you select the best one for your purpose.

GUIDELINES FOR SELECTING CHART FORMS

Graphic Form	Function
Line chart	Change in variables over time
Bar chart	Comparison of variables at one time or several points in time
Divided bar chart	Comparison of variables and their components at fixed times
Pie chart	Relationship of components to each other or to the whole
Diagram	Parts of a process, structure, or unit

Line charts show change over time of one or several variables (see exhibit 8-5).

Exhibit 8-5. Line charts show change over time.

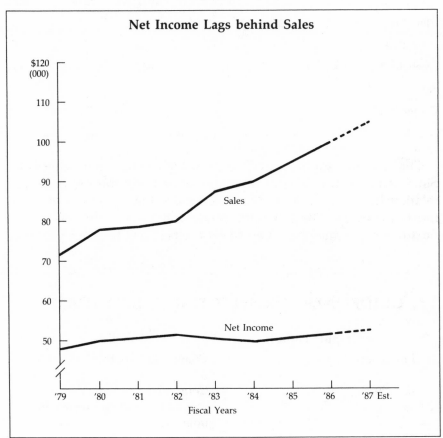

Bar charts, whether vertical or horizontal, are useful in showing the relationship between two or more variables at one time or at several points in time (see exhibit 8-6). Although line and bar charts are frequently used for similar purposes, the line chart is more effective in depicting change over time. The bar chart can either highlight differences between distinct time periods or compare components of a whole at different times (see exhibit 8-7).

Pie charts show the relationship among the parts of a unit at a given moment. Although pie charts are round (as in exhibit 8-8), other shapes can also be used to show parts of the whole. Some

Exhibit 8-6. Bar charts show relationships at discrete times.

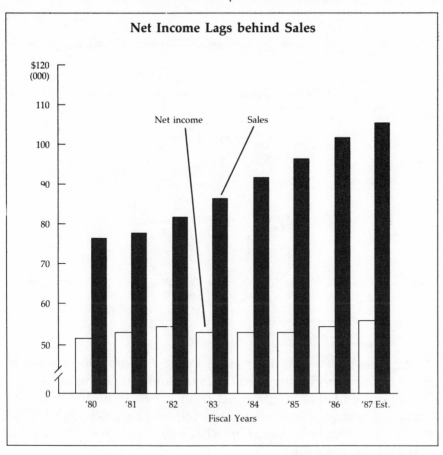

Net Income Lags behind Sales

Exhibit 8-7. Bar charts can show changes of components as well as of the whole.

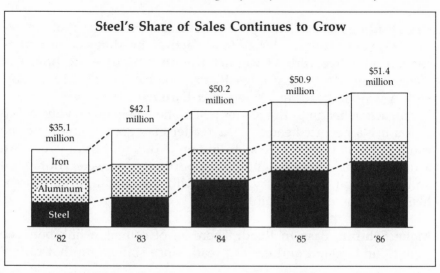

Steel's Share of Sales Continues to Grow

Exhibit 8-8. Pie charts show the relationship of the parts of a whole at a discrete time.

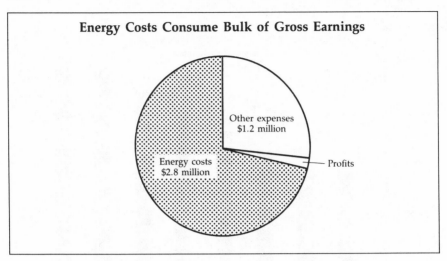

Energy Costs Consume Bulk of Gross Earnings

Other expenses
$1.2 million

Energy costs
$2.8 million

Profits

chartmakers believe that the most important information should be in the section beginning at 12 o'clock and extending clockwise. Others contend that people read from left to right and the most important section should be to the left of 12 o'clock. We believe the decision should be based on what looks best given the amount of data to be presented.

Diagrams, such as organization charts and process charts or flow charts, help the audience visualize relationships and processes.

Use Headings That Convey Your Message. Headings that convey the message are often referred to as "active" headings because they contain an active verb as well as a noun. Compare the power of an active heading, "Earnings Remain Stable as Sales Fluctuate" with a generic heading, "Sales and Earnings, 1980–1986." If you use an active heading, the reader will immediately grasp your point. If you use a generic heading, the reader may get nothing from the exhibit or may come to a conclusion quite different from yours. An active heading provides another opportunity to make your point and keeps you honest. If you start with the heading, the chart is likely to focus on that point.

Make Exhibits Easy to Read. There is, of course, a link between easy to understand and easy to read, since something that cannot be read cannot be understood. But what we mean by easy to read is simple and clear. To be sure your charts are easy to read:

- Eliminate any superfluous graphic features
- Label all critical components

Focus Attention on the Content, Not the Design. Little heads of cauliflower, tanks, or stick figures marching across a page look silly in a management report (some of us think they look silly anyplace, especially when you get down to a quarter of a tank or half a person), and they do nothing to increase the likelihood that the reader will believe your message. Avoid gimmicks. Eliminate as well all unnecessary numbers, lines, and tick marks; make your data more powerful than the graphic design. (See the difference between exhibit 8-9*a* and 8-9*b*.)

For the same reason that you should use only one typeface in a report, you should use only one typeface in your exhibits. Just because the graphics software provides combinations of seventeen fonts in four type sizes and bold, italics, and outlines doesn't mean you should use them. More is definitely not better.

Label Important Components. It is far better to label components on the chart than to force a reader to look at a key. (Compare exhibit 8-10 with 8-6.)

Check for Accuracy

It is easy for typographical errors to slip into text or graphics. Readers, all of whom have made typographical errors at some time or other, are understanding of errors in text. Rarely, we find, are they understanding of errors in exhibits, and there is always someone who will add up the columns to check your math.

In addition, be careful that you do not mislead the audience. According to one theory, for example, British foreign policy was influenced for many years by the fact that the British Foreign Office used only maps of the world that had been prepared on the basis of the Mercator projection, which shows countries nearer the poles as disproportionately larger than countries near the equator. As you prepare your exhibits (and look at charts prepared by others),

Exhibit 8-9. Eliminate distracting elements from charts.

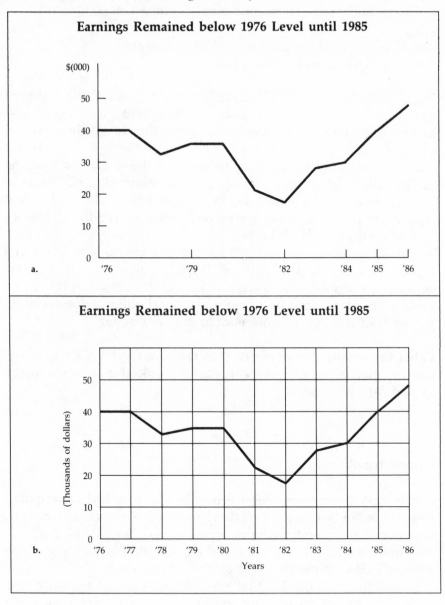

be aware of their potential to deceive. Exhibit 8-11 is an example of a misleading chart. Half-year results should not be set in juxtaposition to full-year results.

Your choice of scale can have a powerful effect on the message

Exhibit 8-10. A key diverts the reader's attention from the data. Compare this exhibit with exhibit 8-6.

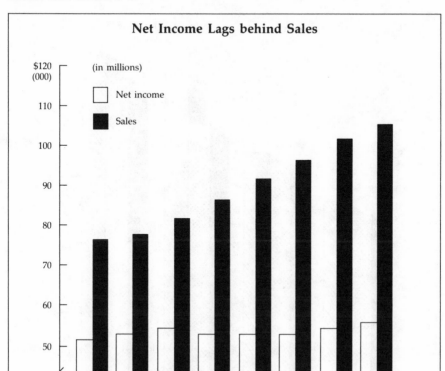

you convey. (See exhibit 8-12*a* and 8-12*b*.) Although your purpose is to persuade, it is to persuade with logic, not with sleight of hand. Check your exhibits to be sure they do not mislead.

Exercise
  Make appropriate charts or tables for the memo you wrote.

SUMMARY

Readability and attractive design are essential to the acceptance of your ideas.

Exhibit 8-11. Charts should show comparable data of equal weight. The half-year data here is confusing and could be misleading.

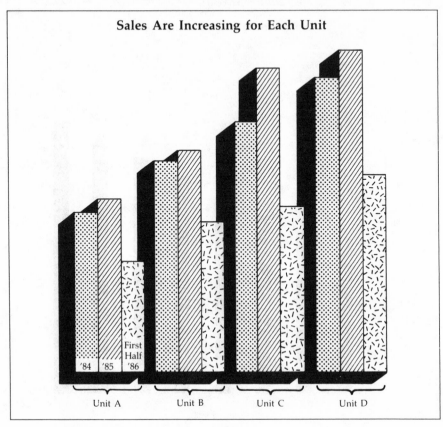

The graphic designs you choose should:

- Focus the reader's attention
- Emphasize the logical development of the argument
- Improve readability

Bullets, white space, underlining, boldface type, and italics all emphasize major points; each has its own purpose and should not be used without thought.

In a long report, headings and subheadings are the best guides for the reader. They should:

- Show the logical development of the argument
- Stand alone
- Be parallel

Exhibit 8-12. Scale influences the impact of a visual.

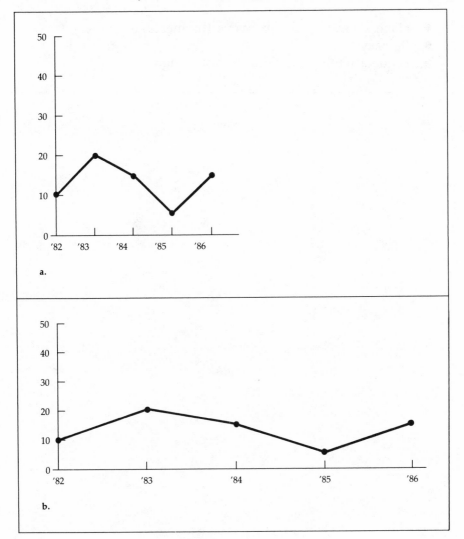

Exhibits are important to the reader because they:

- Present complex material efficiently
- Dramatize major points
- Emphasize relationships

Each visual has characteristics that make it especially useful for conveying specific kinds of information. Be sure to select the most effective form.

Exhibits must:

- Have a heading that conveys the message
- Be easy to read
- Focus attention on content, not design

REVISING IS QUALITY CONTROL

Although deadline pressure may tempt you to skip the revision of your first draft, carefully revising your memo or report always pays off. This chapter will show you:

- How to revise for organization
- How to revise for language

Your secretary has just typed your first draft of a report on the implementation of a new training program for the word processing department. You've spent hours on the thing — interviewing the workers, talking with their supervisors, going over the background of training in that department, laboriously organizing the report — and you probably don't care if you ever see it again. You set a high value on your time, and revision may be one of the steps you can skip. Privately, you view it as sophisticated nit-picking anyway.

But absolute accuracy can be achieved only through carefully checking your prose to make it as clear and concise as possible. If a document is well organized and the language is correct, the reader will be less likely to misunderstand what you are trying to say, to be distracted (or offended) by flagrant errors, or to jump to the conclusion that because you are a sloppy writer you are also a sloppy thinker. Furthermore, even professional writers don't produce a perfect first draft — some of them revise as many as ten times. Except for long reports, you'll probably be able to schedule time for only one revision. But you can't delegate it. Although your secretary may be able to pick up some of your grammatical mistakes, he or she won't be able to spot most errors in meaning. And, although it's legitimate to give a draft of an important memo or report to someone else to read, people are usually reluctant to make comments on someone else's writing. In the end, you are responsible for what you write.

However, revision doesn't have to be a chore. Now that you've started to follow the steps to effective writing outlined in this book — solving the problem, developing a logical organization, and writing a first draft with a view to addressing the reader's needs — you shouldn't have to do wholesale rewriting, throwing out whole sections and starting from scratch. In fact, you should spend less time revising than you did in the past.

Furthermore, revising is rewarding. When you revise, you can make something obviously better with a few minor changes — tightening up sentences by removing vague or unnecessary words, putting a topic sentence at the beginning of the paragraph, making sure that there are appropriate references to exhibits, and correcting headings. And you can spot unnecessary or redundant sections and delete them. In addition, as you begin to learn what sorts of errors you make most often, your first drafts will improve immensely.

Before you begin to revise, let the first draft rest for at least a day — if you're under deadline pressure, overnight will do. If you start to revise immediately after you finish the first draft, you'll be far too involved in what you've been slaving over to evaluate it objectively. Building enough time for revision into your writing schedule will allow you to set a draft aside with a clear conscience.

Revision is a two-step process — reviewing for structural faults and correcting language. The first step is by far the most important. Frequently, if you can find and fix organizational flaws, problems of language and style disappear automatically. For example, convoluted sentences may well disappear when you tighten up the structure.

Revising for Organization

To be a conscientious editor, you have to put yourself in the reader's place. Intelligent readers are responsive. They question as they read. Although you have already checked the organization when you reviewed your tree before you wrote the first draft, asking yourself the following questions will give you a final chance to see things from the reader's point of view.

Does the Structure Jump Out at You? Read through the whole document quickly. Can you instantly tell what the main point is? Is it easy to see what the main supporting points are? If *you* can't find them, knowing everything you know about the subject, chances are the reader won't be able to either.

Is the Purpose Clear? What significance does the main point have for the reader? Does the beginning tell the reader what the memo or report is about, why it is important, and how you will develop the idea? Is it clear what action should be taken on the basis of this piece of writing?

Is the Organization Logical? Check your contents page (in a long report) or your section headings (in a short memo or report) against your tree. Do all points at the same level of importance carry the same weight in the finished document? Does the finished document include all the points you made in the tree? Check your headings: Do all the headings at the same level convey the same sorts of ideas?

Are the Key Paragraphs Well Organized? Is the first paragraph in each section a mini-beginning, answering the **what, why important,** and **how** questions for that section? Remember that the heading is not part of the first paragraph. Many writers open the paragraph that follows a heading with a pronoun that refers to a noun in the heading:

<u>Municipality Will Issue Bonds</u>

They can be a primary source of funds for renovation projects in our region . . .

Because readers do not see the head as part of the text, such vague references will confuse them. Such faults are simple to fix.

<u>Municipality Will Issue Bonds</u>

Tax-free bonds are a primary source of funds for renovation projects in our region . . .

Also check the last paragraph in each section Does it summarize the material in that section or lead the reader into the next section?

Are Your Transitions Accurate? Transitions reveal the relationships among your ideas. Transitions may be words, sentences, or whole paragraphs (in a long report). Make sure they are clear and valid. If you are constructing a deductive argument, for example, you'll want to alert the reader that you are drawing a conclusion by using such words as *therefore, thus,* and *accordingly.* If you are piling up assertions or evidence for your argument, you'll use terms like *in addition, similarly,* and *likewise.* If you are indicating a shift of direction, you'll want to pull the reader up short with *however* or *nevertheless.* Make sure, when you use such words, that they signal a relationship that really exists. Dropping them in at random merely confuses the reader.

Similarly, using the word *this* alone to introduce a new section or paragraph does not provide the reader with enough information. To start out with "This proves beyond a shadow of a doubt . . . ," without saying what *this* refers to, will send the befuddled reader back to the preceding paragraph. You'll often find, when you force yourself to add a noun, such as "this *finding*" or "this *discussion,*" that whatever it is did not prove anything at all.

Do You Keep the Reader Moving Forward? Try not to send the reader back to earlier material in the report with phrases like *as previously discussed.* Similarly, avoid referring to material you will be discussing later in the argument or the reader may skip ahead to see what you are talking about. Naturally, in a long report, you'll include references to the body in the executive summary, and if you have exhibits, they must be referred to in the text. But all material necessary to the argument itself should appear where it will do the most good.

As you check through a draft with an eye to organization, resist the temptation to tamper with the wording. If you see a howler of some kind and it's easy to change, by all means change it. If you will need to go to a thesaurus for a better word or to stop to rewrite a difficult sentence, circle the phrase and keep on going. Circling the offending word or phrase will prevent you from missing it the next time through. But revising for organization and revising for language are separate operations. If you start hacking into the prose while you are revising for organization, you'll never be able to see the forest for the trees.

Revising for Language————————————

Once you've fixed any organizational flaws, you're ready to work on the language itself. Revising for language, grammar, and punctuation is crucial. It's necessary to choose your words carefully because they are your only tools for telling the reader precisely what you mean. A word that means one thing to you may have a totally different connotation for the reader. Legal cases, for example, have been lost because of varying interpretations of a simple word like *speedy*. Although choosing the wrong word seldom has such dire consequences in management, writing "as soon as possible" when you mean "Friday" can lead to trouble.

Punctuation and grammar are equally important because they tell the reader the relationships between words and phrases. If you forget a vital comma or use commas to string together sentences, the reader may have trouble following your ideas and may even have to pause to take stock. Furthermore, inaccurate grammar and punctuation may mislead a reader. Consider the writer who suggested that his store modify its atmosphere "to attract middle-aged women, who are concerned about buying fashionable dresses at low prices." Maybe that's what he meant to say (the comma sets off the clause that follows it, indicating that *all* middle-aged women are concerned about buying fashionable dresses at low prices — something the reader may doubt). It's more likely, however, that he meant the store should try to attract a specific class of middle-aged women — those who are concerned about buying fashionable dresses at low prices. If that was his intention, he should not have placed a comma between *women* and *who*.

There are many good grammar reviews and style manuals, and anyone who writes should have one for reference. It also helps to read aloud what you have written. If you find yourself out of breath, as if you've just run the New York Marathon, you probably need to break up overlong sentences or insert sensible punctuation to provide legitimate pauses. In addition, you'll find that you can actually "hear" many awkward and poorly constructed phrases.

To make your writing immediately clearer and more understandable, you should keep in mind a few simple rules as you review your draft for language:

- Use language assertively
- Construct sentences to show relationships
- Get to the point

- Choose words that work for you
- Use an appropriate tone
- Avoid sexist language

Use Language Assertively

Having confidence in what you are writing and stating it without reservation is as important as satisfying the needs of the reader. In any informal exchange, assertiveness means stating what you want to have happen and why. Just as some people avoid the first person through a mistaken sense that introducing themselves into the written document is somehow impolite or not sufficiently objective, others sprinkle their sentences with qualifying words or phrases like *apparently, in my opinion, it appears,* or *it may.* As a college student dealing with broad topics about which you knew little, you may have gotten into the habit of including such phrases. But as a manager, you should have confidence in what you are saying: you cannot expect your reader to be persuaded by what you write if you hedge everything you say.

Use the Active Voice Whenever Appropriate. To refresh your memory about the difference between the active and passive voice, look at this example:

ACTIVE VOICE: Grand Diamond opened a branch store.
PASSIVE VOICE: A branch store was opened by Grand Diamond.

Compare the two. The active version is shorter and it's clear at the very beginning who is doing what to whom. Organization in sentences is similar to organization in paragraphs and whole reports — tell the reader the most important thing first. In sentences, it's usually most important to find out first who or what is doing something. Compare these two versions of the same sentence:

WEAK: Some confusion is suggested by the data with respect to consumer preference.
BETTER: The data suggest some confusion concerning consumer preference.

Some people in business and government argue that the passive is more polite and more dignified than the active voice. This rationale often simply provides an excuse for obscuring their real meaning or hedging their bets:

WEAK: Sales volume for this year will be lower than previously anticipated.

BETTER: Our department anticipated that sales volume this year would be 25 percent higher than now appears likely.

It's better not to conceal the truth, even if it's unpleasant. In the first place, using the passive to shield the person or department that took the action won't fool anyone. In the second place, telling the reader what actually happened positively and assertively will lead him or her to have confidence in you. It is, however, legitimate to use the passive when:

- The thing or person receiving the action is vastly more important than the person or thing performing the action

  EXAMPLE: President Kennedy was assassinated.

- The person or thing performing the action is unknown

  EXAMPLE: The letter was written anonymously.

- You don't want to cause unnecessary unpleasantness

  EXAMPLE: The Cleveland Index has disappeared from the library. (*Instead of:* Someone has stolen the Cleveland Index.)

Use Action Verbs. Forms of the verb *to be* (*is, are, was*) describe the existence of something. Action verbs describe something that is happening; they give a sense of movement to your writing. In addition, sentences containing action verbs use fewer words than other sentences. Many management writers, perhaps because they lack confidence in their ability to use words that are slightly out of the ordinary, fall back on forms of the verb *to be* or make nouns out of perfectly adequate action verbs. As you edit, you can correct for this habit and give your writing much more vigor in the process.

- Change forms of the verb *to be* to action verbs

  WEAK: There is a feeling among the marketing staff that . . .

  BETTER: The marketing staff believes that . . .

- Change nouns made from verbs back into verbs whenever possible

  WEAK: Marlin's survey established a preference of managers for dealing with a single vendor.

  BETTER: Marlin's survey established that managers prefer to deal with a single vendor.

Construct Sentences to Show Relationships

Writing sentences to show relationships among ideas will dramatically improve the clarity of your writing. Not only does a string of simple sentences make readers catatonic, it gives them no clue as to how the sentences relate to each other. If you don't construct your sentences to create such clues, readers will have difficulty understanding what you're trying to say. Look at this short example:

> The report is well written and concise. It provides a penetrating analysis of the personnel problems that resulted when the staff was reduced by 40 percent over a six-month period. This report will serve managers as a guide. It shows precisely what happened during the six months of the study. The writers challenge the usual view of the corporation's human resources department.

How do the thoughts expressed by each sentence relate to each other? There's no way a reader can tell without stopping to think, which forces the reader to do the writer's work. On careful examination, you can see that the first two sentences relate to each other because they both say something about the characteristics of the report. You might combine them this way:

> The report, which is well written and concise, carefully analyzes the personnel problems that resulted . . .

In this case, you've subordinated the description of the report's style to the idea that it carefully analyzes something. The reader now knows that you consider the report's content more important than its style — a helpful clue. The third and fourth sentences can also be combined in a way that shows their relationship to each other:

This report will provide managers with a valuable guide because it explains events in detail.

The sentence now shows that the value of the report lies in its detailed explanation. As you revise, try to show relationships this way. You might try rewriting sentences several different ways to get a feel for what's possible. If it's appropriate, connecting simple sentences with a coordinating conjunction (*and* or *but*) is better than leaving them to stand alone, but your writing will be much livelier if you try to use such words as *because, since,* and *although* to alert the reader to relationships among your thoughts.

Combining sentences can be carried too far, of course. Some writers overload their sentences with too many ideas:

> Depending on the number and frequency of employees hired, a regularly scheduled training program might be feasible and allow for a more efficient entry process, which would then increase productivity.

The writer obviously was trying to cut down on the length of the sentence, but obscured its meaning in the process. Part of the problem is the passive voice, but this sentence can be fixed easily by making it into two sentences:

> Depending on the number of employees we hire, we should consider setting up a regularly scheduled training program to promote a more efficient entry process. This change would lead to increased productivity.

Mastering parallel structure also shows relationships and improves the clarity of your writing. Parts of a sentence that are parallel in meaning should be parallel in structure. Parallel structure is obligatory when you are dealing with a series of items or actions, because the reader expects that you will demonstrate, by the way you structure the series, that the items are the same. Look at this example:

AWKWARD: The Division has no sales force, no experience in this type of marketing, and is not ready to make its move at this time.

IMPROVED: The Division has no sales force, lacks experience . . . , and is not ready . . .
(Each item in the series starts with a verb.)

You should take special care to use parallelism in lists broken out from the text because mistakes in such lists are painfully obvious.

WRONG: Our product has the following superior qualities:
1. Low cost
2. Multiple uses
3. Our product has potential for acceptance among most market segments.

IMPROVED: Our product has the following superior qualities:
1. Low cost
2. Multiple uses
3. Potential for acceptance . . .

OR: Our product has the following superior qualities:
1. Its cost is low
2. It has multiple uses
3. It should be accepted by most market segments

Get to the Point

Anyone you write to is busy and harassed. If you pile on unnecessary words, phrases, sentences, and paragraphs, the reader will rightly resent your failure to serve his or her needs. Furthermore, your most significant points will be lost in the cloud of words. Saying what you mean economically requires you to eliminate excess words and avoid redundancy (repeating ideas unnecessarily).

Eliminate Excess Words. Most first drafts contain padding. It may be your habit to begin sentences with excess baggage like "the fact that" or "it's possible to conclude that," or "it is my sincere belief that." Writing assertively sometimes eliminates such phrases. Many excess words disappear when you convert verbs to the active voice. You can eliminate others by using verbs instead of phrases to describe verbs:

WEAK: The fact that Ms. Burne is assuming the post of director of operations gratifies me.
BETTER: I'm delighted that Ms. Burne will become our director of operations.

WEAK: It is recommended that this survey be completed four months prior to the shipment of your new equipment.
BETTER: We recommend that you complete the survey four months before we ship your equipment.

WEAK: Those managers who were insecure tended to call fewer meetings than those who were competent.

BETTER: Insecure managers called fewer meetings than competent managers.

Some overblown sentences, of course, must be totally rewritten:

WEAK: We believe that a strategy of concentrating on the "mature shopper" segment represents the most viable choice.
BETTER: Our company should concentrate on the "mature shopper."

WEAK: As per your request to seek a reasonable solution to the problem in the redevelopment project, I would like to offer the following solution to the problem:
BETTER: I suggest we solve the redevelopment-project problem by . . .

Watch out for long strings of unnecessary phrases. Spying these little baggage trains moving slowly through your paragraphs is a sure sign that cutting will improve the pace of your prose — and the reader's understanding.

WEAK: Provision was made *for* the imposition *of* criminal penalties *on* those willfully neglecting their duties *under* the act. *(This fault often accompanies use of the passive. This sentence contains four prepositional phrases — the reader can't grasp the point till he or she comes to the end of the string.)*
BETTER: Under this act, those who willfully neglected their duties were subject to criminal penalties. *(Reduces the prepositions to one in the main clause.)*

Avoid Redundancies. Sometimes repetition is necessary for clarity or emphasis; usually it is a sign of sloppiness or insecurity. Eliminate words that, though different, mean the same thing.

WEAK: You must realize that there is an *established* committee *already in place.*
BETTER: You must realize that a committee already exists. *(Remember, there is no one right way to say anything. Your task is to find the words that come closest to what you want to say.)*

See how concisely you can write this paragraph without losing any of its meaning:

First, the set percentage rate of increase for the health care industry allows a rewarding of institutional inefficiency for those less productive hospitals that have historically operated with a large margin of unwarranted costs. Conversely, those well-managed, efficiently utilized hospitals that have reviewed all areas of operations by department, determined levels of service, and reduced costs appropriately, will be penalized for operating on a narrower margin.

Maybe you came up with something like this:

> The set percentage rate of increase for the health care industry rewards inefficiency. Less productive hospitals will benefit; well-managed hospitals that operate on a narrower margin will be penalized.

You've cut the passage by more than one-half without losing anything essential to the meaning.

Choose Words that Work for You

In most cases there is one word that conveys your meaning most precisely. Frequently, that word is not a multisyllabic monster with a Latin root, but a short word of Anglo-Saxon descent. As you edit, you should be alert to any inaccurate or inexact words that crept in as you were writing.

Watch for Slipshod Usage. Sloppy usage can embarrass you. All the following examples are taken from real memos and reports.

EXAMPLE: Some attention should be given to the size of the room where the processing unit will be located, relative to the heat output and comfort of the operator. *(The heat output . . . of the operator? We've all heard of body heat but . . .)*

EXAMPLE: Management will be satiated by this alternative. *(Not unless it was a longer lunch than usual — the writer means "satisfied.")*

EXAMPLE: The marketing director isolated specific segments of shoppers. *(Not unless he or she goes in for vivisection. Segments are part of a whole.)*

Avoid Jargon, Vogue Words, and Journalese. The meanings of some words are clear only to a specialized audience. You must explain them to anyone else. Other words are overused or misused. A few candidates for immediate banishment, unless used in their original sense, are *factor, dimensions, parameters* (of a problem), *interface,* *impact* (as a verb), *input, options, extrapolate,* and *utilize. Prioritize* and other nonwords may someday become accepted English terms, but until they are you should avoid them as well.

Journalese (sometimes called "elegant variation") shows disrespect for a reader's intelligence. Words like *garner* are seldom seen unless someone gets a sudden urge to liven up his or her prose or has recently been locked in a room with a five-year-old copy of *Time.* Avoid any word you would not use in everyday speech.

Use an Appropriate Tone

Natural writing is effective writing, and readers should be able to see the person behind the printed page. But writers frequently forget that what seems natural to them may be offensive to someone else. Consider your reader's preferences and biases and your own position within the organizational hierarchy to decide whether you should lean toward formality or camaraderie.

Humor is a special case because taste in humor is highly individual. What's hilarious to you may not be even mildly funny to someone else. In addition, humor doesn't travel well. (Have you ever tried retelling a joke you heard on television?) If your communication is passed along, the third person down the line may not know enough about the context to understand the joke, let alone find it amusing. Finally, humor implies that you have a special relationship with the person you are writing to — superiors may consider it presumptuous. It's safer to leave it out if you have any question.

No one wants to be offensive, but even innocent comments are easily misunderstood. An interviewer who compliments a female applicant on her attractiveness may find that she feels he is not treating her professional skills with the respect they deserve. In the same way, people who use ethnic slang and tell ethnic jokes about their own group may be deeply hurt if someone of another ethnic background makes the same jokes. Although humor is sometimes acceptable, discriminatory language and ethnic jokes are not.

Avoid Sexist Language

Sexist language attracts attention these days. Unfortunately, there are no pat solutions, and many recent proposals have outraged language purists. Thoughts traditionally expressed by the third person singular (*his* or *hers, him* or *her*) or substitutes for nouns incorporating *man* or *men* (like *mankind*) present special problems. The following recommendations can help you write memos and reports that are both nonsexist and clear.

Good Solutions. Whenever possible, specify the person you are discussing. If you say Jim Hammock, everyone knows to whom the *he* or *him* in succeeding sentences refers. Use the plural (*they, their,* and *them*). Instead of saying "Everyone should listen to his subordinates," say "Managers should listen to their subordinates." When giving examples, use *she* instead of *he* some of the time. Writing "the executive vice-president" followed by *she* will become easier with practice and may delight your readers. Consistently referring to judges and other power figures as *he* and to subordinates as *she* is distasteful.

An Acceptable Solution. If none of the good solutions is appropriate, it is most useful to say *he or she,* or *she or he* when that can be done comfortably. But don't overdo it. It is ludicrous to write something like this:

> He or she is responsible for making his or her own appointments, so give him or her the program schedule.

You might rewrite the sentence this way:

> Each participant is responsible for his or her appointments and should be given the program schedule.

Nonsensical Solutions. Using *(s)he, s/he* or *she/he* to avoid the awkwardness of *he or she* does nothing about *her or him* or *hers or his.* In addition, this unpronounceable phrase confuses readers who silently say words as they read. Alternating *he* and *she* (and other forms of the pronoun) is nonsense. Consider this example:

> Each person should study his manual daily. It could make a significant difference to her later on.

Whatever solution you choose, you should base your decision on both consideration for the reader's sensitivity and concern for the flow of the language. Any usage that jars or confuses the reader lessens the likelihood that your argument will be thoroughly read, understood, or accepted.

"Male" Words and Other Indiscretions. Without getting into a discussion of such absurdities as renaming manhole covers, we suggest that every writer must be aware of the hidden, and often not so hidden, meanings of some words. Some common terms are demeaning. Secretaries are not *girls*, nor are all working females who are past puberty *working girls*. A man who is employed in a stockroom is a *stockclerk*, not a *stockboy*.

Many words that include the generic *man* can comfortably be changed without changing the meaning: *spokesman* can be *representative*, *workman* can be *worker*, and so forth. Many words, such as *chairperson*, which still sounds strange to some ears, are becoming increasingly acceptable.

Similar qualities in women and men are often described quite differently. A man is called "forthright"; a woman who acts the same way may be termed "abrasive." Slanting your language in this way causes the reader to question your objectivity.

Miss, Mrs., Ms. Again, these social titles are a matter of preference. If you don't know whether a woman is married or single, it is probably safest to address her as *Ms.* If you are writing a letter to someone whom you have met or have spoken with on the phone, ask what form she prefers. Concern for the reader's sensitivity should be the guide.

Exercise
Since revision is extremely important and rewarding, you should now try your hand at it. Revise the memo you are working on, asking yourself the questions in the chapter summary.

SAMPI E REVISED MEMO

A
Delete titles —these
men are on a first-
name basis. See
chapter 2.

To: Hank Berra, ~~President~~

Date: May 29, 1987

From: Sidney Wheaton, ~~Vice-president for~~

~~Personnel~~

Re: Proposed Managerial Training Program

B
Don't hedge — see
chapter 9.

In the past our company /~~appears to~~ *has*

~~have~~ focused almost exclusively on

C
Be specific — see chapter 9.

D
Eliminate excess words — see chapter 9.

E
"And" is inappropriate; the expansion *caused* the demands — see chapter 9.

F
Change passive to active — see chapter 9.

G
Redundant.

H
Parallel structure — see chapter 9.

I
Less is more — see chapter 9.

J
More logical order — see chapter 4.

K
Refer to exhibits in text — see chapter 8.

training programs for clerical and technical personnel. Because of our recent acquisitions, however, ~~positions~~ *the number of* ~~at the~~ managerial ~~level~~ *s* ha~~ve~~ increased *35 percent.* ~~greatly.~~ Many of these positions are filled by people new to management-- systems engineers from DPI, for example. ~~which creates an immediate need for managerial training programs. In~~ *Because* ~~view of~~ our expansion, ~~and the~~ *has placed* growing *demands* ~~responsibilities being placed~~ on ~~our~~ *these new* managers, we must reassess our training programs.

¶ I recommend a two-part program~~: is recommended~~

- Creation of a*n* ~~skills~~ assessment center to diagnose the skills and requirements of new managers and to identify high-caliber recruits

- Institut*e* a six-month *leadership and communications* ~~training~~ program for all new managers ~~This program will stress leadership and communications skills.~~ This program will require a staff of six--two counselors for the assessment center, *and* three trainers ~~and~~ a director. Total cost will be $135,000. *(See attached budget.)*

L
New conclusion
encourages
action — see
chapter 6.

I look forward to meeting with you to discuss this program in detail. Could we set up a 45-minute meeting for the morning of July 2 ?

Proofread Your Memo or Report

Editing your first draft doesn't guarantee that your changes will be made. Typists are human, and you may have given ambiguous directions (typically, people forget to cross out all the words they replace when they make corrections). For anything important, proofreading the final copy carefully is essential. Even minor typos can be embarrassing; some are unintentionally humorous or offensive. Here are some suggestions if you're working alone:

- Don't be afraid to look up a word or phrase in a dictionary or usage book if it "looks funny." You'll often find you were right in the first place — but you'll never catch mistakes if you don't look for them.
- If you find a mistake in a sentence, correct it and then read the sentence again. It's easy to concentrate so hard on the first mistake that you miss an error a few words farther on.
- If a paragraph or section has numerous errors or extensive rewriting, read it aloud from beginning to end. If you're working quickly, you may omit words or forget to delete phrases you've changed. Reading aloud will help you find these slips.

For something that's extremely important, read the entire memo or report aloud to someone — spelling out uncommon words and inserting punctuation.

It's tempting to try to delegate proofreading to your secretary or simply ignore it altogether. But you, the writer, are ultimately responsible for the accuracy of the final document. Don't let all your work preparing and writing a report or memo be marred by carelessness at this stage.

PROOFREADING MARKS

Although you aren't a professional proofreader, using standard proofreader's marks will help your secretary when you are revising and proofreading.

ℑ	Delete, omit word
⌒	Close up
#	Leave space
¶	New paragraph
No ¶	No paragraph
→ or ⌒	Run on. Connects words when space has been left or you have crossed out several lines of text
(more→)	Rest of paragraph continues on next page
⌉⌊	Center
(ts)	Transpose letters or words
(10)	Spell out, don't abbreviate
let it stand	Let it stand (when copy appears to be deleted but you want it to remain)
ℓ̸	Lowercase capital letter
≡	Capitalize lowercase letter
⋀	Insert comma
⋁	Insert apostrophe (or single quotation mark)
⋁ ⋁	Insert quotation marks
⋀	Insert semicolon
⊙	Insert colon
⹀	Insert hyphen

⊙   Insert period

p̶r̶o̶d̶u̶c̶t̶i̶v̶i̶t̶y̶   Make all capitals

SUMMARY

Revising for organization and language requires reading your report or memo at least twice, asking these questions:

- Is the purpose of the document clear within the first few sentences?
- Does the beginning cause the reader to ask the question I want to answer?
- Do I answer that question?
- Is the logical structure of the report or memo clear from reading the table of contents or the headings?
- Are the key paragraphs well organized?
- Is the language forceful? Have I checked for active verbs? Tight sentences? Precise words? No extra words?
- Is the tone acceptable? Have I avoided sexist language?

10

HELPING OTHERS WRITE EFFECTIVELY

Learning to evaluate someone else's writing also helps you become a better writer. This chapter will show you:

- How to appraise writing tactfully
- How to review the writing of your peers and subordinates
- How to review and edit for superiors

It's 4:30 on a Wednesday afternoon. Last Thursday you asked one of your department heads to give you a report on the proposed reorganization of her department by Monday. You'll be using it as part of the monthly report to senior management due this Friday. She just handed you the report with numerous excuses about not having time enough to do proper research, and you're almost afraid to look at it. Hoping you won't be disappointed this time, you start turning the pages. With a growing sense of panic, you realize the report is disorganized, wordy, flippant — there's no way you can submit it without extensive revision. Disgusted, you cancel your earlier plans to go out to dinner with a friend and resign yourself to spending the night whipping the report into shape. You can't afford to be embarrassed by submitting it the way it is.

You should never get to this point. It's true that you frequently have to rely on the work of others when you write lengthy reports, and just as often you may have someone write a memo or letter to go out over your signature. But those writers will be less likely to let you down at the last minute if you help them learn to write more effectively.

Learning to evaluate someone else's writing also helps you become a better writer. As you develop your evaluative skills, you will become more aware of the different ways people express themselves, and learning to "read" people through their writing will help you communicate with them more easily. In addition, by casting yourself in the role of reader instead of writer you will become more sensitive to the needs of a reading audience. Appraising someone else's writing also sharpens your analytical tools so that you can see your own errors more readily. It's easier, after all, to see someone else's deficiencies than to see your own.

Learning to give effective feedback will benefit everyone involved. If you can offer a sensible evaluation of someone else's writing, you and that person will develop a mutual understanding about language and organization — which will in turn decrease the need for further review. Slips in communication skills tend to be incremental. Calling a person on an inaccuracy of grammar or organization the tenth time he or she repeats it is far more difficult than pointing out an error the first or second time: don't put off the inevitable. Although managers are sometimes reluctant to offer suggestions — evaluating any aspect of performance may make both the evaluator and the person being evaluated defensive — mutual confidence depends on effective feedback.

Before you call someone in to discuss his or her work or edit something for a superior, you'll need to appraise the writing itself. Following the guidelines below should help you.

Guidelines for Appraising Writing

Agree on Limits

You may choose to appraise someone else's writing by evaluating, editing, or revising it. Your decision will depend on the nature of the request, if any, and on your relationship with the writer. But be sure to establish, in advance, whether what is required is written or oral comment, minor editing of the original document, or major revision. If you come to agreement on the extent of the appraisal first, you'll avoid the time-consuming game of sending something back, only to have it returned with all your changes ignored.

Read Through Once with a Light Pencil

Before you make any judgments or changes, read the document through making light notes to yourself in the margin if you question anything. Sometimes you find the answer to a question later in a document and are comfortable on the second reading. But the decision makers will read only once; questions should be answered when they arise in the reader's mind. As you go back over the document carefully, refer to your notes and make concrete suggestions.

Find the Main Point

Is it clear what this document is about? In a memo, you should find the main point in the first paragraph. It should be stated specifically and should raise a question, which the rest of the document answers.

Make a Tree of the Argument

Does the writer keep his or her implied promise in supporting the main point? Flip through the communication and find the supporting points for the writer's argument. These should be the topic sentences of the paragraphs in a short memo or the lead sentences of the first paragraphs in each section of a long report. Are these the points you expected the writer to make? Do they adequately support the argument or round out the description? If the argument is complex, diagram a tree for it on a separate piece of paper. Are the sections parallel? Is the argument ordered logically?

Use a Checklist. Use a checklist like the one at the end of this chapter to organize your thoughts so that you can give useful reactions.

Edit Cautiously. If you must write on the manuscript itself, do so in light pencil and try not to make dictatorial comments. Remember that every black mark will remind a writer of unpleasantness in the past — an English teacher, perhaps, who used to proclaim "the pen is mightier than the sword," while obviously wishing for a sword. Resist the urge to use two or three heavy lines to delete a sentence — no one likes to see his words blotted out as if they were an offense to human decency. Avoid exclamation points. If you want to suggest improvements, do so by bracketing the words or phrases that might be left out or changed. Then write your suggestion above. Don't defeat your purpose by writing contemptuous phrases like "Awkward" or "Meaning?" in the margin. Try to recommend a few changes in the wording instead.

Even if you were asked to edit, do not change someone else's words without a good reason. The urge to see your own words in print is enormous. One editor we know keeps this motto prominently displayed: "The strongest drive is not love or hate. It is one person's need to change another's copy." Be wary of this tendency. When in doubt, always query the writer rather than change the words yourself.

Focus on Structure. It is often possible to correct grammar or usage errors by changing the structure of the document. Although many people resist suggestions about grammar or usage on the ill-founded theory that you are inflicting your stylistic whims on them, they may be willing to consider structural changes. It is often easier to demonstrate that a change will make the argument easier to understand than to state flatly that the prose is ungrammatical. For example, someone who splits infinitives thoughtlessly may be persuaded to use another verb form on the principle that the substitute form is stronger.

Be Tactful. If the writer has asked you for written comments, try to start with the large issues and work down to the details. Always remember to phrase criticism as gently as possible. Writing anxiety does exist, as surely as math anxiety does, and harsh criticism may guarantee that the writer will never ask for another evaluation.

Reviewing for Peers and Subordinates

Whatever you were asked to do about someone else's writing, try to talk to the writer about ways of improving rather than returning something with written comments. If your goal is to improve the quality of your staff's writing, meet with each person and share your thoughts about writing habits and practices. Try to schedule the meeting just before giving a writing assignment. This meeting may provide staff members with their only opportunity to learn just what you expect in the way of written communication. They cannot, after all, read your mind; and they may be reluctant to ask questions for fear of seeming ignorant.

Giving Feedback on Drafts

Once you have met with a staff member and discussed precisely what you want, you should provide an immediate opportunity to put the discussion into practice. Try to make the first assignment after your meeting relatively short. The shorter the piece, the fewer problems there are likely to be, and the better chance you will have to avoid defensiveness. You should ask to see a draft or better yet, a tree, rather than a final memo or report. A draft, by definition, is unfinished. Completed memos or reports inevitably contain tiny shavings of the writer's ego — perhaps only a phrase or word he or she thought was especially appropriate, perhaps the entire structure of the argument. If you question such things in a completed document, you may find that you've stepped on a land mine — the offended writer may refuse to accept anything further you have to say.

When you meet with the writer to discuss the draft, keep criticism tactful and constructive. It's not appropriate simply to "dislike" the way a person writes. You must be able to make concrete suggestions about ways to improve. If you have isolated several problems, offer only a few suggestions at a time, usually beginning with suggestions about improving structure. Sometimes simply asking for a shorter version will eliminate a writer's affection for redundancy. Usually, comparing the shorter and longer versions will show the writer that writing can be improved dramatically.

Staff members are also more likely to adopt your suggestions if you can honestly say that you have found certain techniques helpful yourself. You might, for example, mention that you always write an executive summary before you write the first draft of anything dealing with a complicated or technical topic. Or you might show the staff member a tree you developed for something you have written recently. Show someone a report you wrote that went through several revisions to demonstrate that you don't get these things right the first time either. Make it clear that writing is hard work for you, too, but that you have found improving your skills rewarding — and be specific about the rewards.

Strategies for Giving Feedback on Completed Memos and Reports

Sometimes, of course, you won't be able to comment on a memo or report in draft form. By far the best way to give feedback on a final version is to let the piece of writing or the writer provide it for you. If the letter, memo, or report has only minor problems, you can pass it along as is and let the writer take responsibility for it. For example, it you are submitting someone's report as part of your own report, you can make sure that the writer sees the recipient's comments on it. Similarly, if you have a staff member write a letter for you, you might consider letting the writer see the response to the letter, which may demonstrate that the letter didn't communicate as well as it might have. At this point, the staff member may initiate a discussion on ways to improve — the best way for such discussions to start.

If something written for you has serious problems, however, merely passing it along will backfire. You'll be guilty of bad judgment and you'll have to take responsibility for making the writer vulnerable, not an ideal way to establish trust. If serious problems exist, see if you can make it easy for the writer to provide his or her own feedback by asking some nonthreatening questions such as, "How do you feel about this memo or report?" Usually, writers are well aware when they've written something that doesn't make sense, and they'll start a discussion of the gaps or faults themselves. If that doesn't happen, you can try being more specific, by saying, for example: "I'm having trouble understanding exactly what you're saying in this section. Do you think you could explain it to me?" Generally, once the writer starts to explain, he or she will see that there's a communication problem and may even suggest ways to fix it.

Even if the memo or report is totally unacceptable, remember that you aren't doing the writer a favor if you take it upon yourself to rewrite it. A poor writer cannot be expected to learn anything if you do the rewriting. You'll only get another poor piece of writing the next time you give him or her an assignment. Furthermore, doing wholesale rewriting yourself will damage your relationship with the writer — you'll be resentful because of the extra work you had to do and the writer will be angry when he or she finds out about it.

Involving Your Staff Makes Writing More Effective

Whenever possible, involve your staff when you set deadlines for any important project. Writing always takes substantially longer than you believe it will, and setting arbitrary deadlines without consulting your staff members will cause them untold frustration. Don't dash off a memo saying, "I need a report on the Spider account by September 8." First think about precisely what information you need to take action. Write it down. Then call the staff member in and say something like, "Morris, I need a report on the activity in the Spider account quickly, because the marketing manager will be out in Omaha during September and he'll need to know about any complaints. When can you get the report to me?" If Morris says he can get it to you by September 15, ask him if there is any other work he can delay so that he can get it to you more quickly. Taking his workload into account this way makes it more likely that the memo will come in when you want it.

For complicated reports involving several people, you should negotiate the deadline and scope of the project at the beginning to get the most realistic deployment of personnel. You may be requesting something that simply cannot be achieved in the time you set. Make sure that the people involved establish practical intermediate deadlines for the completion of research, outline, executive summary, appendixes and exhibits, first draft, and final copy. Furthermore, although delegation saves you time, it's a good idea to sign off on the outline of the report before the actual writing begins. Catching gross errors of focus and organization at this point will help insure that the final product is acceptable.

Let the people you work with know that you are willing to accept their suggestions about improving your own writing skills. Someone may have been secretly covering for you by correcting simple grammatical mistakes or by adding phrases to clarify your meaning. Encourage your secretary to question anything that does not seem clear. You need this sort of commentary to keep yourself honest. You should also consult with your staff. Ask them if you could change your writing habits in any way that would help them do their jobs more effectively. Ask them if there are any routine writing tasks that you should delegate. Not only will this provide you with valuable information, but asking for suggestions always makes it easier for others to accept your recommendations for improvement.

Progress should be recognized. Once you have given concrete suggestions for improvement, keep track of what your staff members are doing. People are far more motivated by praise than by criticism. For example, when a staff member has cut down the average length of his memos by one-third, with a corresponding increase in clarity, be sure to tell him or her that you are very pleased by this improvement. At the same time, be certain all staff members realize that improving written communications is a continuing process.

Reviewing for Superiors

If all senior executives could write meaningful, well-organized prose, members of their staffs would find life easier. Unfortunately, many senior executives need help with their writing. As you become known as an effective writer, your advice may well be sought by others. You may be called upon to review external as well as internal communications. Editing the writing of superiors is emotionally more difficult than evaluating for peers or subordinates. If you're editing for superiors, be pragmatic. Change obvious errors of grammar and usage if you can cite a rule to support your version; leave intact anything you can without losing your self-respect; question anything you are uncertain about. (Of course, you will not question something you can easily check yourself.) Be sensible. Remember that you don't know for sure what the author was thinking about. Changing "the effect is not unsubstantial" to "the effect is substantial," though it will make a shorter phrase, may alter the writer's meaning. If you can justify a change by claiming that a general reader will not understand what the writer has in mind, or if you can show that there is a grammatical error, the changes will probably be accepted gracefully.

Checking Your Evaluation

Regardless of whether you are revising, editing, or evaluating for a peer, a subordinate, or a superior, success depends on being both flexible and positive. Read first for the structure of the argument, then for appropriateness of tone and language, and finally for overt errors. You can use the checklist given in exhibit 10-1 to review memos and reports written by yourself and others. You will see that the last question on the checklist asks you to consider what

Exhibit 10-1.   Evaluation checklist.

Is the document attractive?
  (Are there generous margins, white spaces, highlighting)

Are there enough intelligently worded headings to indicate the flow of the argument?

Are the parts logically developed?

  Beginning: Is the main point clear almost immediately?

  Do I know why this document is important?

  Do I have an idea how the writer will develop the argument?

  Am I satisfied that I have enough but not too much information to understand the document?

Body: Does the writer answer the question raised by the main point?

Are all my questions answered as they come to mind?

Do I get only the information I need, as I need it? (I don't think "So what?" or "Why are you telling me this?")

Ending: Do I know what the writer wants me to do next?

Do I have a sense of closure (no surprise endings)?

Do the exhibits make the text more understandable?
(Are chart forms appropriate, exhibits attractive, headings active? Has the writer missed opportunities to use exhibits?)

Is the tone appropriate?

What are the most effective characteristics of this document?

was most effective in the document. You cannot answer that question until you have finished reading, but in talking with the writer, you will want to begin with something positive.

SUMMARY

- Learning to appraise other people's writing helps:
  — improve your writing
  — improve your staff members' communication skills
- Always read the document completely before commenting on errors of structure, grammar, language, and tone
- Use tact when appraising someone else's writing
- Choose the best method of giving feedback:
  — comment on drafts
  — let the writing or the writer provide feedback
- Be pragmatic when editing for superiors
- Use a checklist

A NOTE
ON WRITING
ELECTRONICALLY

Do you use a word-processing program to write? Are you part of an electronic mail network? Neither writing at a terminal nor using electronic mail have yet stimulated the changes predicted by computer gurus five years ago. But the potential of each to change spheres of influence in organizations by quickening response time and permitting direct communication among distant individuals makes it important for managers to know how to write electronically.

This chapter will give you hints on:

- Composing on your computer
  — writing quickly
  — revising wisely
- Using electronic mail
  — establishing a system
  — writing for electronic mail

Composing at a Terminal

If you know how to type, writing at a terminal is so easy, once you're familiar with the word-processing program, that you are likely to find yourself resenting the need to use a pencil to compose so much as a note to your secretary. And typing on a computer terminal is fast — it takes less physical effort to touch keys on a keyboard than on a typewriter and somehow knowing that correcting errors is easy frees people to type (keyboard) more quickly. As a result, undisciplined writers may find it hard to stop the flow of words, creating more and more prose until finger fatigue finally stops them. And people who care about language and words admit to spending countless hours massaging their prose, because doing so is easy.

The result is that poor writers continue to produce poor documents and good writers continue to produce good ones and no one, except the secretary, saves much time. What is the solution?

Techniques for Writing More Quickly

The lure of the computer screen, the reluctance to pick up pencil, and the ease with which corrections can be made all encourage a writer to get started. The first lesson to learn about writing at a computer is that it can be a wonderful editing tool, but it is no writing friend.

Organize Before You Write. All the rules set forth in chapters 3 to 9 apply whether you are writing the old-fashioned way, dictating, or working at a terminal — prepare before you write. Using the system for constructing an organization tree, and using that tree as a guide, will ensure that you don't "run off at the keyboard," as one manager called it.

Don't Get Bogged Down over Words and Paragraphs. Some professional writers work successfully by polishing one paragraph at a time. For people who do not write for a living, however, attempting to create the perfect first paragraph may prevent them from ever getting further. In addition, the inability to write notes in the margin makes it very inviting to go back to make a change or insert a new idea. If something occurs as you're writing, try, instead, writing yourself a note in boldface, wherever you are, and go on. If you're one of these writers, force yourself to make an organization tree — and stick to it — every time you write. The alternative, trying to revise as you write, takes time, and it interferes with your thinking process. As you wait for the cursor to reach the right place on the screen, you may forget the sentence you intended to write next.

Don't Use "Canned" or Prepackaged Prose. Although it's tempting to recycle portions of letters, proposals, and reports, remember that canned prose offends people. Moreover, making minor changes in an effort to "customize" fools no one. Just because you have the technical capability of saving these little gems doesn't mean that everyone else will find them brilliant. Furthermore, you may forget to make all the necessary changes. Once the reader sees a reference to another client in your letter, she will know without question that you've made the same pitch before.

Techniques for Editing Wisely

The real value of word processing lies in the ability to create clean copy without retyping. No one need send out a "not-quite-right" document because he fears retyping will introduce new errors, so editing is fairly guilt-free. Check chapter 9 for the basic rules of revision.

Use the Capabilities of the System to Help You

Most word-processing programs have a "search" capability that can help you tighten your prose. For example, ask the computer to show you *-tion*. You may find a fair number of verbs turned into nouns (like *implementation* for *implement*) that you can correct. If you tend to load on such phrases as *the reason is* or *the fact is*, look for *is*, and delete these unnecessary phrases. If you are one of those people who overuse such nonspecific words as *thing*, or writes *this* without a noun, try a global search to check for and eliminate these flaws. Be aware that not every use of a particular word, or part of a word, is an error — the search will show correct usage as well as mistakes. Although time consuming, the search can be illuminating as a periodic check. Searches can help you isolate your weaknesses.

Some programs have built-in counters to tell you the average number of words in each sentence. We don't believe in using these automatically to shorten sentences since the most precise way to say something may require more words than the shorter, more general way. If, however, you tend to write overly long run-on sentences, knowing that your sentences average forty to forty-five words may inspire you to cut down, perhaps by half.

Stop After One Revision

For the language tinkerer, word processing affords the opportunity to play with phrasing and language and tone almost endlessly. Most of us who are guilty of tinkering find that it rarely helps our prose, and frequently makes it stilted. A wise friend once told us, "You never finish a manuscript; at some point you simply abandon it." Surely the same should be true of a memo. Revise once and stop.

Try Different Formats

The appearance of the documents has grown more important as people have become accustomed to looking at print-quality letters and memos. Many word-processing programs and printers offer a large selection of fonts and typefaces. Try different formats and typefaces to see what looks best when you are working on an important document (see chapter 8 for guidelines).

Read Everything in Hard Copy before It Goes Out

The computer screen generally shows only two-thirds of a page at a time, but the reader sees the whole page. Since the way a document looks is often as important as what it says, viewing the document as the audience will see it may prompt you to reformat it. For example, reading hard copy will allow you to create paragraphs to provide white space, keep section headings from appearing to fall off the bottom of a page, and make the use of headings and bullets consistent.

Electronic Mail

Electronic mail, as we define it, is an electronic system of communication in which the writer types the message and sends it to the reader's "mail box," the reader brings the message up on the screen, reads it, and deals with it. Its potential lies in the time it should save both the senders and the recipients.

Five years ago we interviewed users of electronic mail in a range of organizations. Proponents of the new system envisioned a paperless office in the near future and boasted that electronic mail was already raising the metabolism of sluggish bureaucratic organizations. We were told we were looking at the early stages of a revolution.

In talking with users, we found that mail systems were most heavily used by computer people for short messages and that these "writers" had little concern for style or structure. We found some amusing instances of garbled information and heard more than a few stories of insensitive use of language. Difficulty in editing was the most common excuse given for the sloppy language and errors of tone. When "noncomputer people" were put on mail systems, therefore, they were told not to worry about editing, just to "Use it — you'll love it." Among the nontechnical users, more than a few managed to avoid touching a keyboard by using their secretaries as intermediaries. The secretaries turned all incoming messages into hard copy; the managers dictated answers, which their secretaries typed into the system and sent. The time saved in the process was minimal at best.

In 1986 we again conducted informal interviews with managers. Sadly, we found that the world had changed little. The hardware for electronic mail systems, some experts tell us, is collecting cobwebs, and the paperless office is not even on the horizon. Why? Largely, we believe, because of poor planning and lack of training.

Establishing an Electronic Mail System

For electronic mail to be useful,

- Control of the system should be in the hands of users
- Conventions for appropriate use need to be established

Only if the committee or group that controls the form, installation, and use of the mail system is composed largely of users and potential users will the system meet their needs.

One of the errors in installing electronic mail, as people described the installations to us, was the assumption that for the system to be successful, senior people should go on-line first. Because senior people don't write much, however, their terminals languished while potential users with far greater needs waited. Or systems were put in the easiest way possible, simply duplicating formal reporting lines. As a result, these systems frequently connected people who could much more easily talk to each other at the water cooler. A far better design, and the one becoming more common, connects only those people who need to communicate and cannot do so easily, regardless of whether they have a formal reporting relationship.

Although it seems obvious that systems should be easy to use and compatible with existing word-processing systems, few electronic mail systems are either. As a result, users who both write on their terminals and send messages electronically cannot move copy from one system to the other and, in fact, cannot even use the same commands in both systems. Clearly, buyers of systems should be very specific in stating their criteria and demanding that they be met.

Software aside, conventions relating to format, lines of communication, and purpose will need to be established for electronic mail before people will be comfortable transmitting more than short, scheduling messages or the equivalent of a message scratched on the back of an envelope.

Organizations in which writing is the preferred method of communicating have very clear conventions. The stationery used, whether the message is typed or written, the circulation/distribution list — all indicate the tone and kind of communication as well as the position of the writer. Electronic mail systems lack any equivalent conventions. (Electronic mail users have been known to stoop to inserting a parenthetical "Ha-ha" in the text in a pathetic attempt to indicate humor.) Electronic mail could replace any of the traditional means of communication, whether written or spoken. But without a means for indicating where a message falls on the continuum of communications, electronic mail will continue to be viewed as highly informal (a complicated replacement for a phone message), and much of its potential will be lost.

In addition to conventions concerning writing, conventions will be needed to ensure that everyone who needs to be informed is informed. One of the purported benefits of electronic mail is that it is unmediated, that no one interferes in the communication between two people. But support staff, such as secretaries, are thus left out of the loop. To the extent that it is important for them to know what is happening, there must be a mechanism for informing them, short of insisting they read every single chatty message on the screen or in hard copy.

Information overload is as serious a problem as lack of information is. We've been told wonderful stories of users jamming a colleague's files in retribution for excessive copying. And it's awfully easy to clean out your files by indiscriminately sending them to "distribution." The very ease with which materials can be proliferated makes it important that organizations set conventions for FYI mail.

Even with a practical system and established conventions, however, a system can fail if users are not properly trained and do not understand how to make a communication compelling.

Writing for Electronic Mail

A computer screen is approximately two-thirds of a page of paper. Reading on a vertical surface is generally more difficult than reading on a flat surface. And you can't take your mailbox on the 5:52 train. What does all that mean for the user of electronic mail?

Brevity Makes the Difference Between Being Read or Not Read. Recipients regularly demand anything they cannot instantly understand on screen in hard copy; yet they resent the need for hard copy from what is supposed to be an electronic system. If electronic mail is to be the accepted medium for transmitting messages of more than a few lines, the importance of stating your ideas crisply will be increasingly important. If the reader can't find out what you want her to do in the beginning, she cannot flip quickly to the end. And it is easy to "throw away" an electronic communication in frustration; hit the button and it's gone. Making your main point in the first paragraph is vital.

Highlighting Helps the Reader Understand Your Message. Making it easy for a reader to find the major points will be more critical on screen than on paper simply because of the difficulty of reading on the vertical plane. The techniques are the same: bullets, headings, space.

Editing Is Essential. Horror stories are rampant. They range from silly misspellings that resulted in the wrong person showing up for lunch to a full-blown quarrel over some insensitive language. As someone we know put it, "You can't reach into the electronic mailbox and retrieve a message you regret sending." Cooling off before you send a message and rereading carefully are essential.

What about the future? Will we operate in a paperless world? Even the most stalwart supporters of electronic communication agree that we are not likely to give up paper copies altogether, especially in an enormously litigious society. But we are increasingly likely to use computers to span both physical and organizational distances. Thus a manager's original, unrevised message will be read (and judged) by a decision maker who may have never met the writer. The rules for writing electronically are the same as the rules for writing with a pencil and pad: analyze the audience, establish criteria, structure ideas logically using those criteria, and make your main point first. The rewards for following that process rigorously will be even greater for those whose messages appear only on a computer monitor's screen.

APPENDIXES

How to Use the Case Studies

Reading a lot of words about writing is easy, but applying the ideas when you yourself write is more difficult. As a way to test your understanding of the material, and to try out new techniques, we suggest you do the exercises in each chapter, beginning with chapter 2. Doing them will let you work through the writing process for one problem from beginning to end and finish with a well-written, attractively presented memo.

The cases, which are similar to those used in many graduate schools of business administration and public policy, are based on the experiences of real people facing complicated problems. The Complex Assembly Corporation case presents an ethical problem; no numbers are involved. In the Budget Finance Corporation case you may base your answer on the bank's goals alone or you may use the financial data included in the case to support your decision. You may, in the Complex Assembly case, decide not to make a recommendation; in the Budget Finance case you are asked for one. We suggest you read both cases and choose the one that interests you most. If you are ambitious you may try your hand at both.

Because there are no "correct" answers in writing, appendix 2 gives at least two approaches to each exercise. Comparing your responses to those of other managers confronted with the same problem is a valuable way of sharpening your skills.

CASE STUDIES

Complex Assembly Corporation

In late May 1977, John Russo, chief engineer at the Complex Assembly Corporation, sat at his desk shuffling through stacks of test results and notes and puffing on his pipe. Russo, who was sixty-two, had been with Complex for twenty-five years. He enjoyed his work and considered himself part of the Complex "family." Russo had planned carefully for his retirement at sixty-five, and in two years would make the final payment on a forty-two-foot boat, on which he planned to live. Now, if he did not approve the test results before him, he faced the possibility of early retirement.

The Company

Complex Assembly Corporation, with over $100 million in annual sales, was one of the largest U.S. manufacturers of specialty wheel assemblies for heavy machinery. Early in 1977, the company had won the contract to construct nose-wheel assemblies for 300 military aircraft that were being built by High Flying Aerospace Corporation. The contract was important to Complex for several reasons. To minimize the effects of the extreme cycles to which the heavy machinery business was prone, management had for some time been looking for applications of its technology to other industries. But the custom-design nature of its operation was not applicable to any of the mass production markets, and attempts to produce parts for the automobile industry had proved a costly error. In addition, in the early 1970s Complex had been unable to deliver on a contract with High Flying. After a four-month delay, High Flying had cancelled the contract. Not only had Complex lost the $100,000 it had invested in research, development, and testing, but the company had not been able to sell a wheel assembly to any major aircraft producer since.

In its attempt to win the High Flying contract at any cost, Complex had submitted a bid so low that management expected to lose money on the initial sale. However, since wheel assemblies are designed for specific aircraft, replacement parts must be bought from the original builder. Complex expected the initial loss to be minor compared to the income the company ultimately hoped to generate from the sale. Furthermore, if this contract went well senior management expected to earn several million dollars annually in additional sales to other aircraft firms within a few years. When the contract was signed, the division VP called together everyone who was to work on the project and explained its importance to the company. He emphasized the need to do a good job and complete the work on time. Russo had been away on a special assignment during the development of the assembly, but one of the engineers told him that when the VP left, Glen McGoly, manager of the design engineering department, closed the meeting by saying, "Hundreds of jobs are on the line. This contract has to be successful — see to it that it is."

The light-weight wheel assembly that had won the contract for Complex was a new design. Its weight advantage was directly attributable to an innovative ball-bearing housing designed by one of Complex Assembly's most capable engineers, George Simpson. A lanky thirty-five-year-old, Simpson had come to Complex three years before. He was a loner and put in long hours. His work was careful and precise and his superiors recognized him as a "comer." While this was the first aircraft wheel assembly for which he had been solely responsible at Complex, he had previously worked for an aircraft manufacturer. Several other engineers had seen the housing plans and had questioned aspects of the design, but High Flying had approved the specifications.

As designer of the assembly, Simpson was named project engineer for its development. He, in turn, assigned Sam Pilawski to build the test model and to oversee the first tests. (See exhibit A1-1 for Engineering Division reporting structure.) Pilawski, whose engineering degree was in aeronautical and astronautical science, was excited at this opportunity to take on such an important project.

Complex had just ten weeks in which to run the first tests and deliver the first 100 completed assemblies. Because time was a major consideration, the parts for the assemblies had been ordered in quantity before any tests were made. It was Pilawski's responsibility to take the first parts that arrived and develop a prototype assembly that could be used for the initial qualification tests. He was also to oversee the production of the first fifty units from which ten would be chosen for further testing. Qualification tests for military aircraft

Exhibit A1-1.   Engineering Division Reporting Structure

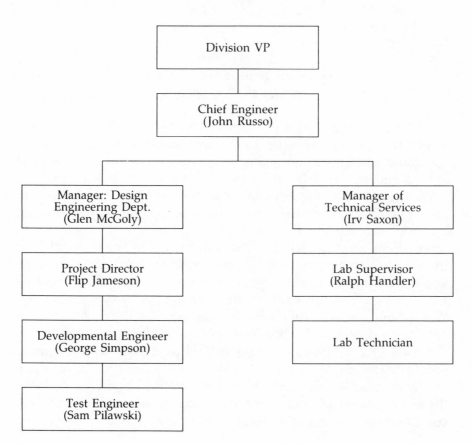

are more extensive than for civilian planes, and High Flying had given Complex very specific and detailed test specifications. The tests fell into two categories, simulated tests at the plant and tests under actual flight conditions at High Flying.

The Tests

Simulated Tests:
- Prototype: 1,000 simulated stops at normal speeds with zero failures;
  100 simulated stops at high speeds with zero failures.
- Ten assemblies chosen at random from first fifty off the line:
  1,000 simulated stops at normal speeds with zero failures;
  100 simulated stops at high speeds with zero failures.

Flight Tests:
- Nine of the ten tested assemblies:
  100 landings at normal speeds;
  50 landings at high speeds.

As soon as the first parts arrived, Pilawski built a prototype assembly and went directly to the test lab with it. The first 100 simulated landings at normal speeds were successful. He was delighted and left the laboratory to tell Simpson the good news.

Within two days the assembly had been subjected to 1,000 simulated landings at normal speeds and the high-speed tests began. Pilawski watched the first ten high-speed tests and was about to leave when the technician called him back. On the eleventh test the wheel assembly froze, causing the wheel to stop turning. Pilawski and the technician quickly dismantled the assembly and found that the bearings and the ball-bearing housing had worn irregularly. When Simpson was called in, he argued that the wear was the result of a defect in the bearings, not the fault of the housing.

It took several days to build a second prototype. This assembly successfully completed the 1,000 stops at normal speeds but froze on the eighty-fifth high-speed landing. Simpson again insisted that the bearings were at fault. The third prototype assembly successfully completed both the 1,000 landings at normal speeds and the 100 landings at high speeds. Curious, Pilawski dismantled the assembly and found that both the housing and the bearings had worn badly. He knew that this assembly could not have survived many additional landings. Although the prototype had passed the test, Pilawski was concerned about the wear on the bearings and the housing and went to Simpson. Simpson stuck to his original position. Noting that the assembly had satisfactorily passed the first portion of the laboratory tests, he demanded that Pilawski order the production of the fifty assemblies from which ten would be chosen at random for the second part of the test. Pilawski agreed to proceed. But he kept the worn housings and the bearings from the first tests in his office. Simpson kept the successful model and returned it to the lab.

Pilawski had ten days between the time he gave the OK for production and the completion of the fifty assemblies. During that period he repeatedly took out the worn ball bearings and housings, looked at them, and replaced them in the cabinet. As soon as the random choice of ten assemblies was completed, in-plant tests began again. All ten assemblies successfully survived 1,000 simulated landings at normal speeds. But only five of the assemblies withstood the 100 landings at high speed. Pilawski went back to Simpson with the results. The five frozen assemblies had irregularly worn housings and bearings. Simpson demanded that the test be repeated. This time it took two weeks for the bearings to arrive, leaving Complex only four weeks before the promised delivery date. Six of the ten assemblies successfully survived a hundred landings at high speed. Meanwhile, Pilawski spent two days alone in his office, making his own computations based on the size, weight, and structure of the bearings and the housings. At the end of that period, he was convinced that the housing was simply too light to survive the stress of continual use. He went to Simpson with his figures. Simpson indignantly insisted, once again, that the problem was a defect in the ball bearing. Since there were now eleven assemblies (five from the first test and six from the second) that had passed the simulated tests, Simpson demanded they select ten of these, and proceed to flight testing.

Convinced that even the successful assemblies would not survive the flight tests, Pilawski decided to go to Simpson's superior, the project's director, Flip Jameson. Jameson, known behind his back as "Flop," had come up the corporate ladder the hard way. Although he had begun work as a draftsman and had no engineering degree, he was in charge of all engineers working on projects slated for production. His position as the supervisor of men with academic credentials far more impressive than his own did not make him popular.

As project director, Jameson was responsible for getting the job done. He had assured High Flying several times that the assemblies had been tested, were successful, and were almost ready for delivery. Now, if he conceded that Simpson's design was not satisfactory, the project would not get out on time, if ever, and Jameson would be responsible to senior management for its failure. He tried to convince Pilawski that there really could be no problem; Simpson was an experienced engineer and obviously knew what he was doing.

Pilawski insisted that they could not send High Flying assemblies that had been selected from two groups of fifty. In frustration, Jameson agreed to one more run of simulated tests.

Simpson and Jameson hung over Pilawski as he prepared for the production of fifty new assemblies. Simpson personally selected each bearing that went into an assembly.

The simulated landing tests at normal speed were again successful. Simpson hung around the lab throughout the testing. On the afternoon the normal-speed tests were completed, he opened the assemblies, examined each of the bearings and housings, and replaced those that looked worn. Pilawski, who found him alone in the lab, objected. But Jameson was "out" and could not be reached; he was the only one with immediate authority to stop Simpson. Pilawski's next step was to approach Ralph Handler, the lab-test supervisor, who would be responsible for writing the test report.

"Look," said Pilawski, "this assembly just isn't going to make it. It's going out there on that airplane and it's going to freeze and everyone in the plane is going to be killed."

Handler was taken aback. "What does my technician say?"

"He wasn't around when Simpson opened the assemblies. The first failures are in the log, of course, but they are all marked 'defective bearing.' He doesn't know about any of this. He is running another set of tests at the same time and he goes back and forth between the two."

Handler pondered the problem. His boss, Irv Saxon, had just had a severe heart attack and probably would not return to the job. McGoly, whose engineers used the technical services division, was taking over temporarily. Handler went to him for advice.

"It isn't so terrible, you know. We've never done anything like this here before, but it's done at other places," McGoly said. "These tests far exceed anything that a plane will normally go through. There simply isn't a chance anything will go wrong in real use. And we're really on the line with this one. If it is successful, there will be promotions here. If not, we may all be out of a job. Let's just get on with it. Time is short."

"What are you going to do about it?" Pilawski asked Handler after the meeting with McGoly.

"If they want a qualification report, I'll write one. But I have to tell it like it is," Handler said. "No false data or false reports are going to come out of this lab."

"Then how can you let Simpson run tests after he's fiddled with the bearings?"

"I'm not his boss," Handler retorted. "I only write reports, I don't run tests."

On the high-speed test, nine of the wheel assemblies survived 100 landings. On the evening before the tenth assembly was to be tested, Handler found Simpson checking the housings and bearings. Simpson said it was a routine check. The assembly passed the test.

"That's it," Simpson said. "Let's get going with that report."

"You know what that report's going to say," Handler reminded him. "I don't tell anything that isn't true."

"You don't have to," said Simpson. "You have ten assembly units that passed the test."

"But you tampered with one."

"I was only checking it out of curiosity. The log doesn't show any changes."

Handler realized that was true, since the log was kept by the technician. At that point McGoly entered the lab.

"Champagne for everyone. We've passed the test — Complex is on its way to the top again. Ralph, you'll have a division of your own soon."

Handler had taken the job at Complex in order to make his wife happy. She had not been well and had wanted to return to the town in which she had grown up, and to her parents. Complex was the only place in town where he could do the work for which he was trained. What would happen to his family if he refused to sign the report, he wondered.

Pilawski simply couldn't believe the whole thing. The test results, with Handler's signature and McGoly's approval, were on their way to Chief Engineer John Russo's desk before the assemblies went to High Flying for flight testing.

Pilawski decided he had to get to Russo before the test results did. He told Russo the whole story and showed him the original worn bearings and housings and his own and Simpson's calculations. Russo, who had extensive experience in wheel-assembly design, quickly saw the flaw in Simpson's calculations and the weaknesses in the housing. However, Russo also knew that the wheel assemblies were due at High Flying in two days for flight tests and that the first 100 production models were due in two weeks. He knew if they opened the ten assemblies going to High Flying, and changed any worn bearings and housings, there was virtually no chance that any of the assemblies would freeze during the test flights.

Russo thanked Pilawski for the information and said he'd get back to him. He then took his notes from the meeting and went across the hall to his good friend Susan Wish, a marketing expert who had "grown up" with Russo at Complex. He told Wish the story and the two considered the wheel-assembly calculations. Finally, Wish turned to Russo.

"Look, John, you're sixty-two and you're going to retire in three years. You have a forty-two-foot boat waiting for you and you're anxious to take off for the Caribbean. What are the alternatives? We all know the tests on these assemblies far exceed anything that any plane normally experiences. All of the tests at normal speeds were satisfactory. It's really very unlikely that anything will ever go wrong. If the worn housing and bearings are replaced on the tested assemblies, the flight tests should go just fine. The top brass thinks that this contract is important and everyone along the line has approved the tests. If you don't sign, you're going to have to go out on a limb for your position. If you do that, and people go along with you, we will lose a contract and people here will lose jobs. If people don't go along with you, you'll have no choice but to resign. That plane probably won't be in use for a couple of years, anyway, and it's always possible that they'll alter the whole assembly before then."

John Russo returned to his desk. He had to decide what to do.

Budget Finance Corporation————————————————

On December 8, 1972, John Lerue sat in his office at a major New York bank holding company. At nine the next morning he was to meet with the corporation's investment committee to discuss a proposed $1.2 million loan to Budget Finance Corporation. He was new to his job and had not yet decided what to recommend to the committee or what data he wanted to present in the form of exhibits. He began, again, to review the proposal, both in terms of the bank's interests and Budget Finance's potential for success.

Finance Industry Note

Finance companies buy paper (accounts receivable) from retail firms and use that paper as collateral to secure loans from a factor or bank, using that money to buy more paper. A simple example should make the economics of the industry clear: Company A pays $75 for $100 worth of accounts receivable. It then takes the note for $100 to a factor or bank, and borrows $100 at 12 percent. Even if the factor or bank deducted the interest in advance, Company A would have $88, with which it could buy $117 worth of accounts receivable. In reality, the finance company deducts its interest in advance by purchasing accounts receivable at some percentage of face value, while the bank or factor generally collects interest over the period of the loan. Purchasers of the goods frequently default on payments. Thus, the percentage of face value that a finance company will pay for a note depends on the risk of default and the interest rate the bank or factor charges the finance company.

The Proposal

Early in 1972, Robert Ephram, president and principal owner of Budget Finance, had proposed to Lerue that the bank buy $1.2 million in convertible debenture bonds from his company. Budget was in the business of buying paper from small retailers who sold furniture and household goods in low-income neighborhoods in the greater New York area. Ephram believed he had developed a system that would increase the percentage of purchasers who actually made all payments under the terms of their credit agreements with the retailer. He argued that the bank should grant Budget the $1.2 million loan, both because it was a good business deal and because the loan was in line with the bank's commitment to support businesses in low-income neighborhoods.

The Bank's Commitment

The bank had substantial loans outstanding to small businesses in all parts of the city. Since late 1968, however, management had prided itself on making a high proportion of the bank's loans in low-income neighborhoods and advising small businessmen in these areas on financial matters. During late 1971 and early 1972 the bank had conducted a "Street Program," in which representatives of the bank — branch officers and public relations personnel — had gone into poor neighborhoods to explain banking and good business practices to groups in schools and to business associations. Senior management considered this effort good business as well as a civic duty, since it was anxious to protect the loans made in these neighborhoods. Bank advertising, in newspapers and on television, emphasized management's desire to help ghetto entrepreneurs.

Because the bonds that Ephram proposed that the bank buy could be converted into common stock, the bank might, at some future time, share in the ownership of the company.

The Budget System

When Ephram and Lerue first met, Ephram had outlined in detail his plan to decrease the percentage of defaults on loans in low-income areas. As he explained the problem, the prevailing financial arrangements reflected the retailers' lack of commitment to the customer. The retailers' principal interest was in delivering the merchandise and submitting the contract to a finance company. As most of the retailers dealt in only one product and repeat business was uncommon, there was little incentive to keep the customer happy. The moment the sale was concluded the retailers felt that their relationship with the customer was over. This attitude, according to Ephram, led retailers to adopt a number of questionable sales techniques that contributed to customers' unwillingness to pay for merchandise:

1. **Misleading promises**
   Salesmen, particularly those who sold merchandise door to door, often made unrealistic claims about the value of merchandise.
2. **Poor quality products**
   Many of the products sold by these companies were of poor quality, although prices were considerably higher than for equivalent or better products in a department store.
3. **Lack of service**
   Although salesmen and advertising literature extolled the virtues of follow-up service and repair facilities, these facilities were often inadequate to meet demand and frequently were located in places customers were not able to get to.

In addition, Ephram maintained that retailers did not actively seek down payments. As long as they could sell their paper at a reasonable discount to the finance company, down payments were relatively unimportant. Salesmen frequently contributed part of their sales commission to the down payment, making up their losses through increased sales volume. Ephram believed a customer who made no down payment had little or no commitment to ownership.

Ephram went on to claim that between 1968 and 1970 Budget had developed a system to counter these problems. The company:

1. Agreed to purchase all contracts from the retailers with whom it dealt
2. Insisted on a minimum down payment of 20 percent for purchases made by a new customer
3. Advanced the retailer only 50 percent of the total purchase price, holding the remainder in a special Dealer Reserve Account. The retailer was paid by Budget as payments were received from the customer
4. Provided management, administrative, and accounting services to assist the retailer
5. Provided merchandising assistance by arranging loans to help retailers broaden their product lines
6. Established minimum standards of quality for merchandise sold by retailers with whom it worked
7. Served customers through bilingual communications
8. Represented the customer when he or she received faulty merchandise

In the written proposal that Ephram had delivered to Lerue, he made the following claims about the unique qualities of Budget Finance:

1. **A Trained Management Team**
   Whereas most finance companies our size have three or four low-salaried employees, we have built up a management team that has had broad experience in all phases of our corporate activities. Members of the management team have backgrounds in finance, administration, and sales, gained both in small companies and in multinational organizations.
2. **Fully Computerized Operation**
   In our business it is essential to have absolute control over Accounts Receivable at all times to detect default trends by dealer. We have dedicated considerable time and money to developing computer programs that will track accounts by type of merchandise and location. The use of random access storage in the computer will vastly increase

our control capabilities. It is our ultimate intent to receive daily management statements from our data processing center.

3. **Large Company Concept**

   Even though Budget Finance Corporation was family owned in its early years, we insisted on audited statements. We have legal advice from a major New York law firm. Personnel has been trained to absorb and handle additional responsibilities. Controls exist to verify and check the handling of incoming funds. All our thinking has been in terms of a large organization.

4. **Limited Delinquency Losses**

   Most finance companies do not withhold sufficient dealer reserves. For these companies, any losses beyond those expected represent direct operating losses. Under the Budget concept, the finance company is only affected adversely if the total losses exceed 30 percent of the paper purchased, because the dealer's reserve account is charged for bad debts. Thus, the downside factor is very limited.

5. **Established Retailer Responsibility**

   We finance the cost of merchandise for the retailer; his profits and overhead are obtained out of the collection of the accounts receivable. The retailer receives needed cash and the customer is served better because the vendor is committed to perform his part of the bargain until the last cent is collected.

6. **Specially Trained Personnel**

   Our personnel have been specially trained to handle the problems of minorities and economically deprived persons. We have hired persons of Hispanic descent and maintain close contact with retailers of Latin American origin. All our communications with the Spanish-speaking community are in Spanish and our Spanish dunning notices are not merely verbatim translations of our English notices, but are indeed "Spanish" notices.

In 1972, when Ephram came to Lerue with his proposal, the Budget Finance system had been in effect for two years and the company had approximately $2 million in receivables. Budget factored these receivables through a commercial corporation. Ephram was anxious to consolidate the company debt and build a line of bank credit, which would be less costly.

The Principals

Ephram's ability as a salesman impressed Lerue. He believed that Ephram's charm would attract retailers, who would prefer to deal with him rather than with smaller, less supportive credit agencies.

In addition, Lerue believed owners of small businesses would be convinced by Ephram's arguments that they would actually make more under his system than by dealing with the standard loan companies. Ephram had ten years of experience in the finance business.

Ephram's partner, who had been born in Buenos Aires, had spent five years as a coffee futures broker and fifteen years as an accountant and banker. He understood the financial aspects of the business and served as a link to the Spanish-speaking community.

The National Economy

The year 1972 had been one of economic growth, and in December economists were optimistic about 1973 and the long run.

The issue of *Business Week* that had arrived on Lerue's desk that morning included the following 1972 data:

Housing starts for November up 10 percent from November 1971

Personal income for November up 10.5 percent from November 1971

Wholesale and retail inventories for October up 6 percent from October 1971

Lerue made these predictions for 1973 based on the projections of a group of leading economists:

Real growth in GNP	5 percent
Price increases	4 percent
Average unemployment	5 percent

The stock market had broken 1,000 during October, and analysts on Wall Street concurred that business would be good and unemployment would not exceed 5 percent for at least two years. Lerue saw no reason to anticipate an economic decline over the short term.

Although there had been some talk among bankers during the past week that a credit crunch was possible within the next twelve months, his bank's senior economist had told Lerue that morning that he did not agree with those prognoses. The prime rate was 5.5 percent and he anticipated little increase.

New York Economy

New York had been slower to recover after the 1968–1969 recession than had other parts of the country. Few of the ghetto areas of the Bronx had been rebuilt and large portions of the borough were, in Lerue's words, "a wasteland." The lack of economic growth in New York had been blamed, by many, on business's unwillingness to build in an area in which the skilled labor force was declining rapidly. The nonwhite population of the city continued to grow, and middle-class whites were moving to the suburbs in increasing numbers. Lerue had been responsible for loans to medium and small businesses in all five boroughs of New York and he knew the owners were barely breaking even. In spite of the optimistic projections for the nation, Lerue felt less sanguine about the economic future of New York.

Lerue agreed with Ephram's argument that the primary market for time-payment purchases in New York would continue to grow and he accepted Ephram's estimates that in 1972 the Budget "market" extended to 1.5 million buying units in New York and New Jersey and that each unit had an annual disposable income, for furniture and capital goods, of $400.

Of the many documents included with the proposal to the bank, Lerue was especially interested in the income and expense figures (see table A1-1). As he considered what recommendation to make to the investment committee, he chose to view the conversion part of the proposal as attractive but unlikely. He did not believe the bank was interested in going into the finance business. He viewed the bonds as a straight 10 percent loan.

Budget Finance Corporation
Comparative Expense and Income Analysis

FORECAST, EXPENSES
Actual (1968/69–1971/72) Forecast (1973/77)
(in thousands of dollars)

	68/69	69/70	70/71	71/72	1973	1974	1975	1976	1977
Salary Expenses	100.0	152.3	168.4	196.0	290.8	576.0	945.0	1353.0	1839.0
Office Expenses									
Rent[1]	2.1	2.9	2.4	4.6	6.0	36.0	78.0	120.0	120.0
Telephone	11.8	21.6	20.3	16.6	25.9	56.0	96.0	150.0	226.0
IBM[2]					12.0	36.0	36.0	36.0	60.0
Office Supplies[3]	26.1	35.2	29.7	30.5	16.0	24.0	36.0	60.0	80.0
Depreciation	3.1	2.7	3.1	3.5	1.0	3.0	5.0	7.0	10.0
Miscellaneous	12.9	28.8	14.7	8.8	21.0	38.0	64.0	84.0	108.0
Office Expenses	—	—	—	—	5.0	8.0	9.0	9.0	11.0
SUBTOTAL	56.0	91.2	70.2	64.0	113.3	259.0	414.0	632.0	887.0
Administrative Expenses									
Professional Fees	6.4	11.2	12.3	20.9	36.0	36.0	48.0	60.0	78.0
Travel/Enter-tainment[4]	10.1	10.8	10.0	15.6	22.5	54.0	84.0	108.0	162.0
Auto Expenses	6.2	2.7	3.1	4.8	8.0	24.0	24.0	24.0	24.0
Miscellaneous	0.7	1.7	1.3	0.1	12.0	24.0	24.0	36.0	48.0
SUBTOTAL	23.4	26.5	26.7	41.4	78.5	138.0	180.0	228.0	312.0
TOTAL EXPENSES	179.4	269.9	265.3	301.4	482.6	973.0	1539.0	2213.0	3038.0

FORECAST, INCOME
Comparative Income Analysis
(in thousands of dollars)

	68/69	69/70	70/71	71/72	1973	1974	1975	1976	1977
Interest & Disc. Earned[5]	385	589	484	430	409	1,817	3,792	7,018	11,008
Premium Income[6]	17	31	31	31	13	67	158	310	458
Charges to Dealers[7]	27	19	35	5	54	127	237	386	541
Other Income[8]	—	—	26	13	27	86	249	485	1,014
TOTAL INCOME	429	639	576	479	503	2,097	4,436	8,199	13,021

1. The increase in rent beginning in 1974 is based on anticipated expansion needed to meet business growth.
2. IBM charges beginning in 1973 and increasing in the next year are based on expansion of the data processing system.
3. Includes stationery, postage, office supplies, and data processing (1968–72).
4. The increase in travel and entertainment expenditures is based on the institution of management seminars and education programs for retailers and members of the Budget staff.
5. Indicates the income from the loan of money to the purchaser; controlled by the usury laws of the states involved.
6. Time payment arrangements include life insurance and accident and health insurance. A portion of the premiums of these policies is paid to Budget by the insurance company.
7. The retailer is charged a $10 fee per contract for a credit check.
8. These monies come from late charges and other services, such as accounts receivable management, outside consulting services, and specialized services like mailings and auditing, which the company provides for dealers.

SOLUTIONS TO CASE STUDY EXERCISES

This appendix contains several approaches to the Complex Assembly case questions and the Budget Finance case questions. All of the Complex Assembly answers appear first, chapter by chapter. When there are two responses, those marked "**a**" refer to a memo to the division vice-president, and those marked "**b**" refer to a memo to Pilawski. For the Budget Finance case, those responses marked "**a**" refer to a memo recommending making the loan, those marked "**b**" refer to a memo recommending against making the loan.

Complex Assembly Corporation

Chapter 3

a. Russo, whatever his decision, will have to notify his immediate superior, the division vice-president.

AUDIENCE PROFILE

Who is the decision maker or primary reader?

Division Vice-President

What question did or might the decision maker ask?

What should we do about wheel assemblies?

How much credibility do I have with the decision maker?

Lots — he trusts me

How much does the decision maker know about the subject?

Nothing about the tampering

What is the decision maker's view of the subject?

Believes contract is crucial to Complex Assembly

What is the decision maker's managerial style?

Likes short memos

Who will influence the decision maker? What do they know? How might they react?

Possibly CEO, Board of Directors
No knowledge

What question do I want to answer?

What should we do?

What do I want the decision maker to do?

Send assemblies

Should I write or speak?

Rather talk, but must write

b. To Pilawski.

AUDIENCE PROFILE

Who is the decision maker or primary reader?

Sam Pilawski

What question did or might the decision maker ask?

What are you going to do about the assemblies?

How much credibility do I have with the decision maker?

Lots—his boss

How much does the decision maker know about the subject?

Everything

What is the decision maker's view of the subject?

We should not send assemblies

What is the decision maker's managerial style?

(Doesn't apply)
Personal style — conscientious, persistent

Who will influence the decision maker? What do they know?
How might they react?

(Doesn't apply)

What question do I want to answer?

What will you do?

What do I want the decision maker to do?

Accept my decision.

Should I write or speak?

Sensitive subject: better to speak,
but need written record.

Chapter 4

In analyzing the question "Should I accept the test results and send the assemblies?" Russo might choose to draw two analysis trees: one considering the possibilities if he sends the assemblies (exhibit A2-1) and one considering the possibilities if he does not send them (exhibit A2-2). Russo might select the following criteria against which to judge his alternatives.

Nonnegotiable Criterion	Reason
Not endanger human life	Ethical judgment

Negotiable Criteria: (ranked on a scale of 1–5 with 5 the most significant)

Criteria	Weight	Reason for Weight
Preserve image of reliability	5	All future contracts are dependent on maintaining a reputation for completing contracts close to schedule
Avoid loss of High Flying contract	4	Loss of this contract will cost jobs and will hurt the company's image
Not result in loss of my job	4	I need the remaining years of income to fulfill my retirement dream
Not hurt Pilawski	2	He is a good engineer, but can get another job

Russo might view the nonnegotiable criterion this way:

Sending the assemblies would put a test pilot's life in jeopardy. Therefore we should admit to High Flying we have failed.

Or he might view it this way:

The chance that a life will be lost is nil. Therefore I can consider the alternatives in terms of the negotiable criteria.

Exhibit A2-1.

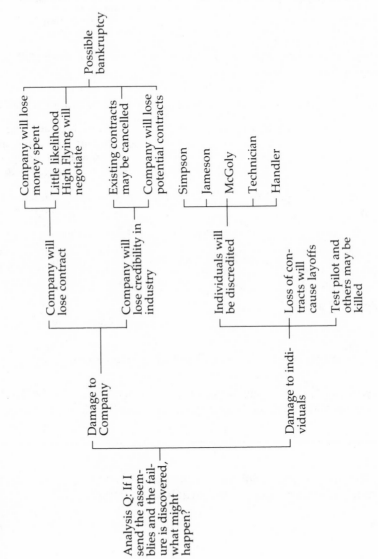

Analysis Q: If I send the assemblies and the failure is discovered, what might happen?

Damage to Company
- Company will lose contract
  - Company will lose money spent
  - Little likelihood High Flying will negotiate
    - Possible bankruptcy
- Company will lose credibility in industry
  - Existing contracts may be cancelled
  - Company will lose potential contracts

Damage to individuals
- Individuals will be discredited
  - Simpson
  - Jameson
  - McGoly
  - Technician
  - Handler
- Loss of contracts will cause layoffs
- Test pilot and others may be killed

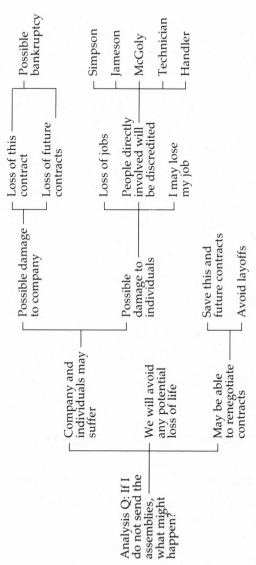

Exhibit A2-2.

Analysis Q: If I do not send the assemblies, what might happen?

- Company and individuals may suffer
  - Possible damage to company
    - Loss of this contract
    - Loss of future contracts
      - Possible bankruptcy
  - Possible damage to individuals
    - Loss of jobs
    - People directly involved will be discredited
      - Simpson
      - Jameson
      - McGoly
      - Technician
      - Handler
    - I may lose my job
- We will avoid any potential loss of life
- May be able to renegotiate contracts
  - Save this and future contracts
  - Avoid layoffs

a. He might then continue this way:

ALTERNATIVE: SEND THE PARTS

Criteria	Value	(× Criteria = Weight)	Reason
Preserve image of reliability (5)	2	10	I believe the news of the test failure will ultimately get out
Avoid loss of High Flying contract (4)	3	12	We can probably get away with this long enough to reconstruct the faulty part
Not lose my job (4)	4	16	Time is on my side
Not hurt Pilawski (2)	0	0	No chance of convincing him
Total score		38	

ALTERNATIVE: DON'T SEND THE PARTS

Criteria	Value	(× Criteria = Weight)	Reason
Preserve image of reliability (5)	5	25	News of the failure will ultimately get out
Avoid loss of High Flying contract (4)	0	0	If we don't send parts, we will lose contract

Not lose my job (4)	0	0	Top management is dedicated to the success of this product
Not hurt Pilawski (2)	5	10	He will be delighted
Total Score		35	

b. Or this way:

ALTERNATIVE: SEND THE PARTS

Criteria	Value	(× Criteria = Weight)	Reason
Preserve image of reliability (5)	0	0	We will be found out
Avoid loss of High Flying contract (4)	4	16	We will complete contract and make changes that will avoid suit
Not lose my job (4)	4	16	I can convince management I wasn't responsible
Not hurt Pilawski (2)	0	0	He will not understand
Total score		32	

ALTERNATIVE: DON'T SEND THE PARTS

Criteria	Value	(× Criteria = Weight)	Reason
Preserve image of reliability (5)	3	15	Should be able to convince industry our rejection shows reliability
Avoid loss of High Flying contract (4)	1	4	Unlikely we can renegotiate
Not lose my job (4)	4	16	I think I can convince them I wasn't responsible
Not hurt Pilawski (2)	2	4	He will be delighted, but will suffer personally
Total score		39	

Chapter 5

a. Exhibit A2-3 shows Russo's organization tree for his memo to the division vice-president.

b. Exhibit A2-4 shows Russo's tree for his memo to Pilawski.

Exhibit A2-3. Memo to the Division Vice-President

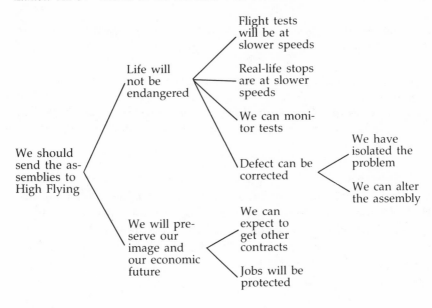

Exhibit A2-4. Memo to Pilawski

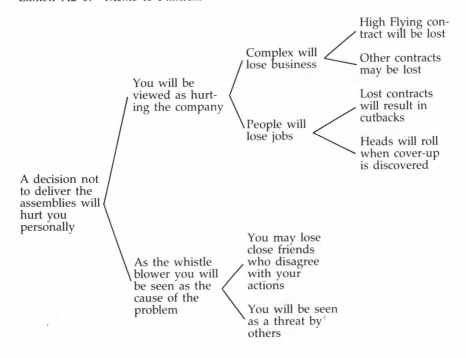

Chapter 6

a. Russo might begin a memo recommending sending the assemblies this way:

> After four weeks of prototype production and laboratory tests, we must now decide whether to forward the wheel assemblies to High Flying for flight testing. Ordinarily, the decision would be clear-cut. However, in going over the test results, I found certain problems, including unusual wear in certain parts.

Although no one likes to be the bearer of bad news, Russo's coy allusion to "certain problems" will not earn him points with the division vice-president. Although Russo may want to protect his people, this contract is crucial, and the vice-president will not want to wait until page 2 to find out what went wrong. The following opening paragraph tells the vice-president what went wrong and recommends action.

> The wheel assembly tests for the High Flying contract are now complete. However, the results reveal that landings at high speeds may cause unexpected wear in parts of the assembly. In spite of this finding we should not delay sending the assemblies (**what**). They are serviceable at normal landing speeds, and delay will severely damage Complex's financial status and reputation (**how**).

Note that there is no **why important** in this opening statement. The vice-president surely knows that this contract is the most important thing to happen to the company this year. Telling him about its importance yet again might be viewed as patronizing.

b. Russo might write the beginning of a memo to Pilawski this way:

> Sam, I am writing to you for two reasons.

> I have decided not to approve the assembly, and to recommend that we renegotiate our contract based on further strengthening of the assembly. You should be aware of the ramifications of my decision, and how these may affect you. The major effects are the potential financial impact this decision will have on the company and on the personal lives of your co-workers.

Although Russo indicates in this beginning that some problems are in store for Pilawski, he does not say why he thinks so. Pilawski will probably be puzzled by this subtle approach. In a memo based on a deductive argument, the writer should start with the more general idea. In addition, using "Sam" in the beginning may indicate a closer relationship than Russo intends to maintain with his subordinate, even though Russo is trying to get across the idea that "we're all in this together." The following opening is more effective:

> Thank you for sharing with me your misgivings about the safety of the High Flying wheel assembly. I have decided not to approve the test results (**what**). Although I know this decision will please you, I am concerned that you may suffer personally as a result of it (**why important, how**).

Chapter 7

First Draft
a.

```
To: VP Production
From: John Russo
Re: High Flying Contract

    The wheel assembly tests for the High Flying contract are
now complete. However, the results reveal that landings at
high speeds may cause unexpected wear in parts of the
assembly. In spite of this finding we should not delay
sending the assemblies. They are serviceable at normal
landing speeds, and delay will severely damage Complex's
financial status and reputation.
    Although there has been some criticism of the way the tests
were handled, the wheel assembly, as it stands, will meet the
requirements of actual flight testing at High Flying.
Simulated tests always exceed the actual requirements of
real-life use. In actuality, any plan landing at the speed
simulated in the high-speed laboratory test would overshoot
the runway and crash regardless of the strength of the wheel
assemblies. As a result, the flight tests will occur at
slower speeds that the simulated tests and there was no signs
of wear in the assemblies in simulated tests at these speeds.
```

Furthermore, we can take precautions to monitor the
conditions of the assemblies that we send on to High Flying.
Our technical representatives will dismantle the wheel
assemblies after every actual flight test to assure that we
have not made mistakes in our calculations.

To take care of the design defect my engineers are working
on a way to upgrade the assembly's strength while remaining
within the High Flying's design specifications. We have
isolated the problem and hope to rectify it shortly. The
improved assembly can be phased in immediately.

Although we could opt to delay sending the assemblies, the
consequences would be severe. We must preserve our image as a
reliable supplier of high-technology parts. All our future
business depends on this. If we postpone sending the
assemblies, we will once more have failed to meet our
contractual obligations. The immediate result will be loss of
High Flying's business. Severe though the economic
consequences of this loss may be in terms of layoffs and
plant closings, they will be nothing compared with our loss
of face in the defense industry. If we fail this time, all
doors will be closed to us.

b.

To: Sam Pilawski
From: John Russo
Re: High Flying Wheel Assembly

Thank you for sharing with me your misgivings about the
safety of the High Flying wheel assembly. I have decided not
to approve the test results. Although I know this decision
will please you, I am concerned that you may suffer
personally as a result of it.

You are aware, I am sure, that a person who brings a
problem to light is often seen as the cause of that problem.
We may lose the High Flying contract. This can mean extremely
tough financial times in the short run as much of our growth
has been planned around the successful completion of this
contract and the opening of new markets which we hoped would
ensue. Many, especially those in senior management, view this
contract as essential to the life of Complex. In addition,
our reputation and therefore long term business may be lost.

The lives of your co-workers may be seriously affected by
the loss of the contract. This means a loss of promotions, a
possible closing of career options, and most significantly a
loss of work for many in the Complex family.

I realize that you did not create the problem and I admire your courage and perserverance in pursuing it. I do feel however that I should warn you that you may lose friends as people will see you as threatening their job security. I trust you will successfully handle what may be a rather unpleasant situation.

Chapter 8

Some memos do not lend themselves to the use of headings. The draft of the memo from Russo to Pilawski in chapter 7 is quite short and therefore does not need headings. The memo from Russo to the division vice-president is also short. Furthermore, it presents an argument that the writer might not care to have "jump off the page." For examples of good uses of headings, see the revised memos for the Budget Finance case in this appendix.

Chapter 9

Revising the Memo
a.

To: VP Production

From: John Russo

Re: High Flying Contract

The wheel assembly tests for the High Flying contract are

now complete. However, the results reveal that landings at

high speeds may cause unexpected wear in parts of the

assembly. In spite of this finding we should not delay

sending the assemblies. They are serviceable at normal

landing speeds, and delay will severely damage Complex's

financial status and reputation.

~~Although there has been some criticism of the way the tests~~ ¶

~~were handled,~~ the wheel assembly, as it stands, will ~~meet the~~

pass the

~~requirements of actual~~ flight testing at High Flying. #

create greater stress than flight tests or

Simulated tests ~~always exceed the actual requirements of~~

actual

~~real life; in actuality,~~ use; any plan**e** landing at the speed

simulated in the high-speed laboratory test would overshoot

the runway and crash regardless of the strength of the wheel

assemblies. ~~As a result, the flight tests will occur at~~

the Our tests did not reveal any irregular wear

~~slower speeds that the simulated tests and there was no signs~~

in the wheel assemblies

~~of wear in the assemblies in simulated tests~~ at these speeds. *slower*

Furthermore, ~~we can take precautions to monitor the~~

~~conditions of the assemblies that we send on to High Flying~~

Our technical representatives will dismantle the wheel

at High Flying   in

assemblies after every ~~actual~~ flight test to ~~as~~sure that ~~we~~

are   mistaken.

~~have~~ not ~~made mistakes in~~ (our calculations)

~~To take care of the design defect~~ my engineers are working

correct   design = defect without

on a way to ~~upgrade~~ the ~~assembly's strength while remaining~~

violating   the   of the contract.

~~within the High Flying's design~~ specifications. We have

correct

isolated the problem and hope to ~~rectify~~ it shortly. The

as soon as it is ready.

improved assembly can be phased in ~~immediately.~~

failing to

Although we could ~~opt to~~ delay sending the assemblies, ~~the~~

meet the contract deadline   disastrous.

~~consequences~~ would be ~~severe.~~ We must preserve our image as a

reliable supplier of high-technology parts. All our future

it.

business depends on ~~this.~~ If we ~~postpone sending the~~

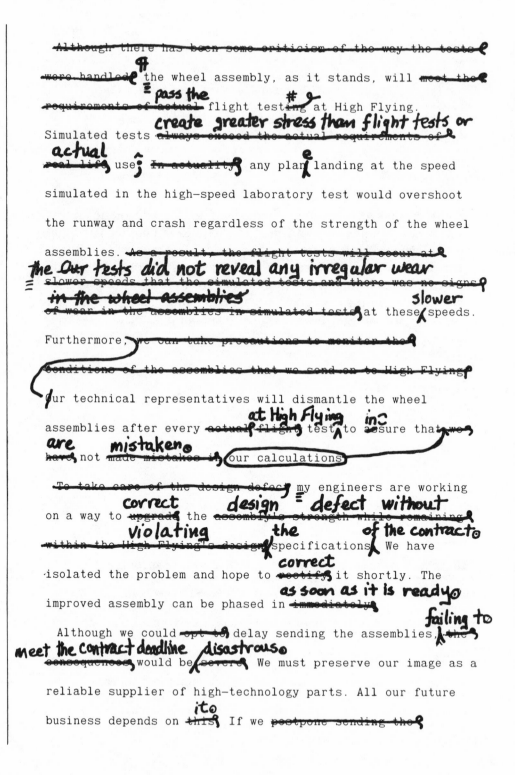

~~assemblies, we will once more have~~ failed to meet our
this time:
contractual obligations. The immediate result will be *the* loss of
High Flying's business. Severe though the economic
consequences of this ~~loss~~ may be in terms of layoffs and
the long-term effects
plant closings, they will be nothing compared with ~~our loss~~
loss of ~~reputation~~ *business if we forfeit our reputation for*
~~face in the defense industry.~~ If we fail this time, all
doors will be closed to us.   *(reliability)*

To: VP Production
From: John Russo
Re: High Flying Contract

   The wheel assembly tests for the High Flying contract are
now complete. However, the results reveal that landings at
high speeds may cause unexpected wear in parts of the
assembly. In spite of this finding we should not delay
sending the assemblies. They are serviceable at normal
landing speeds, and delay will severely damage Complex's
financial status and reputation.
   The wheel assembly, as it stands, will pass the flight test
at High Flying. Simulated tests create greater stress than
flight tests or actual use; any plane landing at the speed
simulated in the high-speed laboratory test would overshoot
the runway and crash regardless of the strength of the wheel
assemblies. The tests did not reveal any irregular wear at
these slower speeds. Furthermore, our technical
representatives will dismantle the wheel assemblies after
every test at High Flying to insure that our calculations are
not mistaken.
   My engineers are working on a way to correct the design
defect without violating the specifications of the contract.
We have isolated the problem and hope to correct it shortly.
The improved assembly can be phased in as soon as it is
ready.

Although we could delay sending the assemblies, failing to meet the contract deadline would be disastrous. We must preserve our image as a reliable supplier of high-technology parts. All our future business depends on it. If we fail to meet our contractual obligations this time, the immediate result will be loss of High Flying's business. Severe though the economic consequences of this may be in terms of layoffs and plant closings, they will be nothing compared with the long-term loss of business if we forfeit our reputation for reliability. If we fail this time, all doors will be closed to us.

b.

To: Sam Pilawski

From: John Russo

Re: High Flying Wheel Assembly

Thank you for sharing with me your misgivings about the safety of the High Flying wheel assembly. I have decided not to approve the test results. Although I know this decision will please you, I am concerned that you may suffer personally as a result of it.

As you probably realize, ~~You are aware, I am sure,~~ that a person who brings a problem to light is often seen as the cause of that problem. Because of your report, and my decision, (complex) loss ~~We~~ may lose the High Flying contract. This can ~~mean extremely~~ severely damage the company ~~tough financial times~~ in the short run, ~~as much of our growth~~ we have expanded to produce these assemblies and to enter the ~~has been planned around the successful completion of this~~ new markets the High Flying contract would open ~~contract and the opening of new markets which we hoped would~~

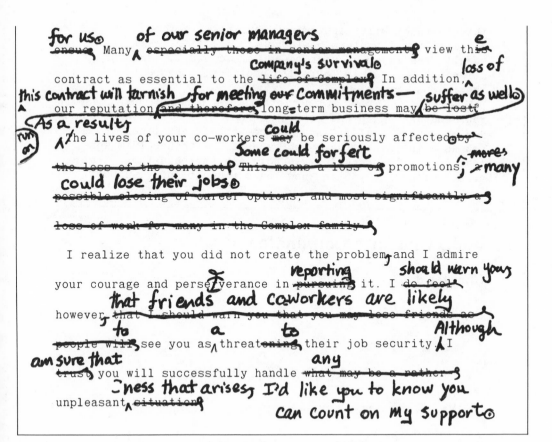

(Edited draft with handwritten revisions)

~~ensure~~ [for us.] Many [of our senior managers], ~~especially those in senior management,~~ view th~~is~~[e] [company's survival.] contract as essential to the ~~life of Complex.~~ In addition, [loss of] [this contract will tarnish] our reputation ~~and therefore~~ [for meeting our commitments —] long-term business may ~~be lost~~ [suffer as well.]

[As a result] [run on] The lives of your co-workers ~~may~~ [could] be seriously affected ~~by the loss of the contract. This means a loss of~~ [Some could forfeit] promotions; ~~many~~ [mores] [could lose their jobs.] ~~possible closing of career options, and most significantly a loss of work for many in the Complex family.~~

I realize that you did not create the problem, and I admire your courage and perseverance in ~~pursuing~~ [reporting] it. I ~~do feel~~ [should warn you] however, ~~that I should warn you that you may lose friends as~~ [that friends and coworkers are likely] ~~people will~~ [to] see you as [a] ~~threatening~~ [to] their job security. [Although] I ~~trust~~ [am sure that] you will successfully handle ~~what may be a rather~~ [any] unpleasant ~~situation~~ [-ness that arises;] [I'd like you to know you can count on my support.]

To: Sam Pilawski
From: John Russo
Re: <u>High Flying Wheel Assembly</u>

Thank you for sharing with me your misgivings about the safety of the High Flying wheel assembly. I have decided not to approve the test results. Although I know this decision will please you, I am concerned that you may suffer personally as a result of it.

As you probably realize, a person who brings a problem to light is often seen as the cause of that problem. Because of your report, and my decision, Complex may lose the High Flying contract. This loss can severely damage the company in the short run; we have expanded to produce these assemblies and to enter the new markets the High Flying contract would open for us. Many of our senior managers view the contract as essential to the company's survival. In addition, loss of

this contract will tarnish our reputation for meeting
commitments--long-term business may suffer as well. As a
result, the lives of your co-workers could be seriously
affected. Some could forfeit promotions; many could lose
their jobs.

I realize that you did not create the problem, and I admire
your courage and perseverance in reporting it. I should warn
you, however, that friends and co-workers are likely to see
you as a threat to their job security. Although I am sure
that you will successfully handle any unpleasantness that
arises, I'd like you to know you can count on my support.

Budget Finance Corporation

Chapter 3

Lerue might have focused on his reader as shown below.

AUDIENCE PROFILE

Who is the decision maker or primary reader?

Investment Committee

What question did or might the decision maker ask?

Should the bank make this loan?

How much credibility do I have with the decision maker?

Little; new man

How much does the decision maker know about the subject?

Nothing about Budget

What is the decision maker's view of the subject?

Committed to increasing visibility in low=income areas

What is the decision maker's managerial style?

Likes brief reports — lots of numbers

Who will influence the decision maker? What do they know? How might they react?

No one.

What question do I want to answer?

Should we make the loan?

What do I want the decision maker to do?

a: make the loan   b:don't make the loan

Should I write or speak?

Both

Chapter 4

To answer the question of whether the bank should buy the debentures, Lerue must first decide if the investment is sound — if the company will be able to repay the debt. He might develop the tree shown in exhibit A2-5 as the basis for his research. Or

Exhibit A2-5.

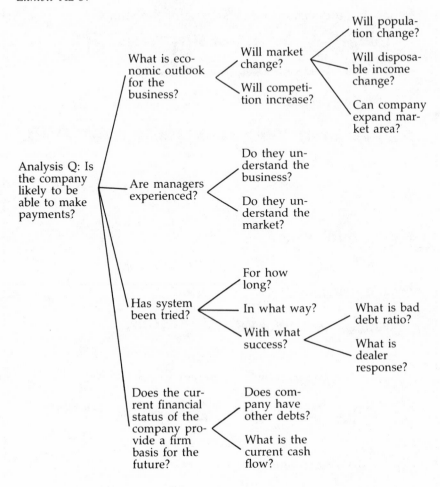

Lerue might develop an analysis tree based on what he believes are the bank's criteria for making a loan (see exhibit A2-6).

Lerue might establish these criteria:

Nonnegotiable Criterion	Reason
The company will not default in the foreseeable future.	Bank policy

Negotiable Criteria: (ranked on a scale of 1–5 with 5 the most significant)

Exhibit A2-6.

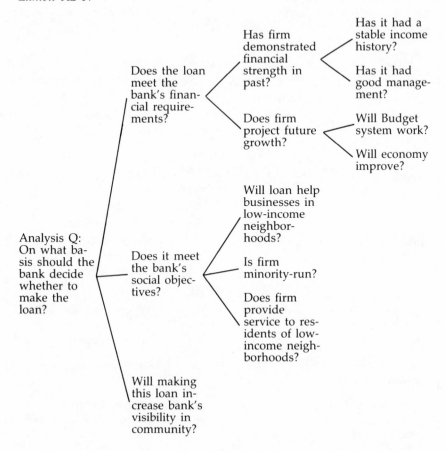

Criteria	Weight	Reason for Weight
The investment must increase bank visibility in the community	5	Senior management is committed to participating in development of low-income communities in ways that improve the bank's image
The company will keep an average monthly balance of $100,000 in checking account	3	We are not, currently, as concerned with balances as with community visibility
Financial ratios are not currently below industry averages.	2	We have been accepting below-average ratios regularly from low-income area businesses.

| The investment must help companies in low-income neighborhoods. | 4 | Bank is committed to helping the community grow. |

a. Lerue might decide that he accepts Ephram's figures and that analysis shows the company will not default on the loan. Since the loan meets the nonnegotiable criterion, he would continue:

ALTERNATIVE: MAKE LOAN

Criteria	Value	(× Criteria = Weight)	Reason
Investment will increase visibility (5)	5	25	We can develop billboard and TV advertising with principals
Company will keep adequate average balances (3)	3	9	At first, company will need all the available cash to expand
Financial ratios meet industry average (2)	0	0	Ratios don't equal industry average
Investment will help companies in community (4)	4	16	Support for this company will filter funds to other neighborhood businesses
Total score		50	

In this instance, if there are no better alternative uses for the funds, Lerue would recommend making the loan since not making it would have a total score of zero.

b. If Lerue decides the proposal does not meet the nonnegotiable criterion, he does not need to continue the analysis. Even if the loan does meet this criterion, if it has a low score (as it does in the following evaluation), he may choose not to recommend it.

ALTERNATIVE: DENY LOAN

Criteria	Value	(× Criteria = Weight)	Reason
Investment will increase visibility (5)	2	10	Potential for advertising is small
Company will keep adequate average balances (3)	0	0	Record shows Budget does not have enough cash to maintain balances
Financial ratios meet industry average (2)	0	0	Ratios don't equal industry average
Investment will help companies in community (4)	0	0	This loan will not help other businesses
Total score		10	

Chapter 5

Lerue might picture his argument supporting the loan as in exhibit A2-7. In arguing against the loan, Lerue might develop the tree shown in exhibit A2-8.

Chapter 6

a. Lerue might write this beginning for the memo recommending that the bank make the loan:

Some months ago, Robert Ephram approached me with the proposal that the bank purchase $1.2 million of convertible debentures in Budget Finance Corporation, a small-loan company with offices in several low-income neighborhoods in the greater metropolitan area. He argued that the loan fits our advertised goal of participating in the revitalization of these neighborhoods. I have worked with him on the development of the financial data before you, and I believe that such a loan can be

Exhibit A2-7.

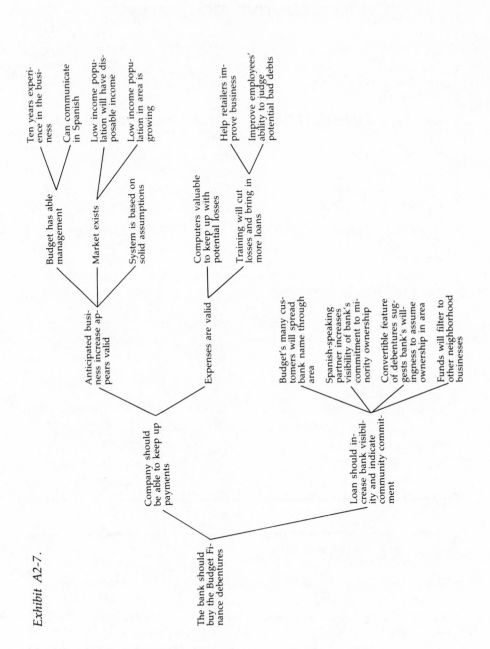

Exhibit A2-8.

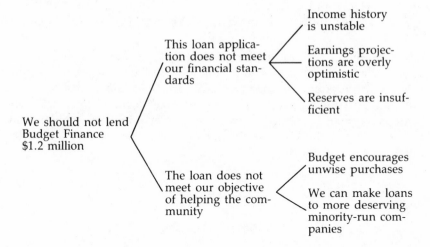

We should not lend Budget Finance $1.2 million

This loan application does not meet our financial standards
- Income history is unstable
- Earnings projections are overly optimistic
- Reserves are insufficient

The loan does not meet our objective of helping the community
- Budget encourages unwise purchases
- We can make loans to more deserving minority-run companies

supported on the grounds that it meets both our financial and social criteria.

Looking at it critically, Lerue could decide that the Investment Committee is not interested in how long he had been meeting with Robert Ephram or in the nature of Ephram's arguments. He would then rewrite the beginning this way (fixing some of the wording at the same time):

> At its next meeting, the Committee must decide (**why important**) whether to approve the purchase of $1.2 million of convertible debentures in Budget Finance Corporation, a financial services company that buys commercial paper from retailers in low-income neighborhoods (**what**). I recommend that we approve this loan: it both meets our financial criteria and advances us toward our advertised goal of participating in the revitalization of low-income areas (**how**).

b. For his modified outline memo recommending against the loan, Lerue might start out with a simple one-sentence introduction:

> I recommend against making a $1.2 million loan to Budget Finance Corporation.

Because he is distributing this memo to the committee members just before the meeting and will make a presentation, he may think he can fill in the gaps verbally. Furthermore, the committee will know why the subject is significant — they are, after all, meeting to make a decision on it. He might decide, though, that he should build some credibility, and rewrite it this way:

> Based on my analysis of the Budget Finance Corporation financial statements, my meetings with Robert Ephram, Budget's president, and my view of the economic future of New York, I recommend that we do not purchase the $1.2 million in convertible debentures (**what**). The company's financial record does not meet our minimum standards for investment and the loan would not meet our objective of aiding the minority community (**how**).

Chapter 7

First Draft
a.

To: Investment Committee
From: John Lerue
Re: Budget Finance Loan

At its next meeting, the Committee must decide whether to approve the purchase of $1.2 million of convertible debentures in Budget Finance Corporation, a financial services company that buys commercial paper from retailers in low-income neighborhoods. I recommend that we approve this loan: it both meets our financial criteria and advances us toward our advertised goal of participating in the revitalization of low-income areas.

Budget Finance should be sufficiently strong to meet the payments on the debentures. Anticipated business increases appear valid based on the strength of management and on the growing market. With ten years experience, Ephram has developed a program that should attract retailers to do business with him. He seems to have judged the problems of the industry well and to have established ways to overcome the past problems of shoddy merchandise, poor follow-up on bad debts and poor selection of potential customers. In addition, the bilingual experience of employees, and particularly the bilingual abilities of one of the principals, should bring in new business.

At the same time, the market is expected to improve. As the population in the neighborhoods where Budget is based grows and as welfare payments increase and the general level of employment improves, there should be substantially more disposable income in the area.

Although the figures indicate that Budget's expenses are quite high relative to income for the next few years, these expenditures should provide the base for further income growth. The installation of new computers should help limit the losses that are considered a part of this business by permitting management to keep abreast of any changes in the economy that affect its market. The training expenditures planned by Budget will serve both its employees and the retailers with whom the company does business. The retailers should improve their business, and therefore Budget's income, through this training and the company employees should be in a better position to judge poor prospects as a result of this experience. The combination of management experience, solid systems, well-spent training and computer funds, and a growing economy should provide Budget with more than enough funds to repay its debt to the bank.

At the same time, making this loan will increase the bank's visibility in the low-income areas where the company is situated and indicate our commitment to helping the community grow. The size of the Budget operation permits us exposure in almost every area in which we are interested. And as the company grows that exposure will increase. We anticipate some joint advertising that should serve us both well. We have been looking, for some time, for a chance to participate in an organization that has a Spanish-speaking partner. In addition, the convertible feature of the debenture will suggest to the community that we have an interest in owning property in the area.

The training programs Budget will run will have a ripple effect in the community as other organizations gain from their exposure to Budget's ideas and as Budget provides funds to retailers that will increase their sales.

The loan will serve the bank and will serve the community.

b.

To: Investment Committee
From: John Lerue
Re: Budget Finance Loan

  Based on my analysis of the Budget Finance Corporation
financial statements, my meetings with Robert Ephram,
Budget's president, and my view of the economic future of New
York, I recommend that we do not purchase the $1.2 million in
convertible debentures. The company's financial record does
not meet our minimum standards for investment and the loan
would not meet our objective of aiding the minority
community.
  This loan does not meet normal standards for investment.

  - Budget Finance's income history has been unstable.
  - The company's income and expense projections are
    unrealistic.
    --Expense projections are massive.
    --Income projections are unrealistic.
  - Budget's reserves are insufficient to weather any
    economic downturn.
    --Even with this loan, Budget will be undercapitalized.
    --Although the national economic outlook is excellent,
      New York City, particularly the area in which Budget
      operates, may not share in this growth and may even
      suffer a further economic erosion.
    --Although Budget has an impressive management team,
      their expertise cannot compensate for the first three
      deficiencies.

  This loan does not meet our objective of aiding the
minority community.

  - The Budget system encourages minority residents to
    purchase shoddy merchandise on credit at inflated
    prices.
  - The $1.2 million could be divided among several better-
    run businesses in the community.
    --We have requests pending.
    --We can seek new prospects.

Chapter 8

Most frequently, writers add headings as they revise. The answers to the chapter 9 exercises include a revised memo with headings.

a. If Lerue were making a recommendation for the loan, he might want visuals with these headings:

1. Budget expenses, although high, will contribute to earnings.
   (Line graph of expenses and income projections.)
2. Budget locations are near bank branches.
   (Map showing area Budget serves and bank branch locations.)

b. If Lerue were making a presentation supporting a memo recommending against making the loan, he might want visuals titled as follows:

1. Budget Finance's income history has been unstable.
   (Bar chart showing income since firm's founding.)
2. Budget projections are unrealistic.
   (Overlay to first chart showing projected income.)

Chapter 9

Revising the Memo
a.

```
To: Investment Committee

From: John Lerue

Re: Budget Finance Loan

   At its next meeting, the Committee must decide whether to

approve the purchase of $1.2 million of convertible

debentures in Budget Finance Corporation, a financial

services company that buys commercial paper from retailers in

low-income neighborhoods. I recommend that we approve this

loan: it both meets our financial criteria and advances us
```

toward our advertised goal of participating in the revitalization of low-income areas.

(margin note: underlined, not ital.)

Budget's Application Meets Our Financial Criteria

Budget Finance should be ~~sufficiently strong~~ able to ~~meet the~~ make payments on ~~the debentures.~~ schedule. The ~~anticipated~~ increase in anticipated business ~~increases~~ seems reasonable, given Budget's strong ~~appear valid based on the strength of~~ management and ~~on the~~ projected growth. Drawing on his ~~growing~~ market, ~~with~~ ten years' experience, Ephram has developed a program that should attract retailers ~~to do~~ and ~~business with him. He seems to have judged the problems of~~ His new system should overcome ~~the industry~~ 's traditional problems — ~~well and to have established ways to overcome~~ ~~the past problems of~~ shoddy merchandise, ~~poor~~ inadequate follow-up on defaults, ~~bad debts,~~ and poor selection of potential customers. In addition, ~~the~~ his bilingual ~~experience of~~ partner and employees, ~~and~~ ~~particularly the bilingual abilities of one of the principals,~~ should ~~bring in~~ attract new business in the Spanish-speaking community. ~~At the same time,~~ retail ~~the~~ market is expected to improve as ~~the~~ retailers serve population in the neighborhoods ~~where~~ Budget ~~is based grows~~ in the area grows and as welfare payments ~~increase~~ and ~~the general level of~~ increase employment ~~improves, there should be substantially more~~ disposable income in the area should keep pace, justifying Budget's forecasts.

Although ~~the figures indicate that~~ Budget's expenses ~~are~~ will be ~~quite~~ high relative to income for the next four (see Exhibit 1), ~~few~~ years, these expenditures ~~should provide~~ will lay the ~~base~~ foundation for further income growth. The installation of ~~new~~ computers should help limit the losses ~~that are considered a part of this~~ usually associated with the finance business ~~by~~ ~~permitting management to keep abreast of any changes in the~~

The proposed training programs will help retailers improve their business practices and give company employees the expertise to make informed decisions and weed out poor prospects. The company's management experience, innovative programs, combined with training and computer systems, and a easily growing economy should provide Budget with the cash flow necessary to repay its debt to the bank.

The Loan Will Aid the Minority Community

At the same time, this loan will be a visible symbol of the bank's commitment to helping the low-income areas where the company is involved. The size of Budget permits us to have a branch (see Exhibit 2) in almost every neighborhood. And as the company expands, our exposure will also increase. Joint advertising, both print and TV, will reinforce this tie.

In addition, because the debentures are convertible, acquiring them will demonstrate the bank's interest in ownership of local business and the loan itself.

Budget's training programs will have a ripple effect in the community as retailers will improve their management skills, and Budget will channel the bank's funds

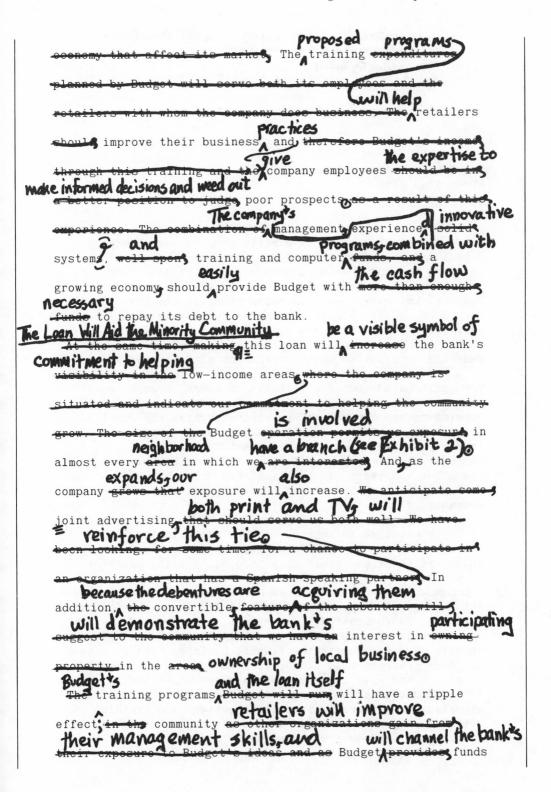

to retailers~~that will increase their~~ sales. *indirectly contributing to their increased*

The loan will serve the bank and will serve the community. *to Budget, then;*

To: Investment Committee
From: John Lerue
Re: Budget Finance Loan

At its next meeting, the Committee must decide whether to
approve the purchase of $1.2 million of convertible
debentures in Budget Finance Corporation, a financial
services company that buys commercial paper from retailers in
low-income neighborhoods. I recommend that we approve this
loan: it both meets our financial criteria and advances us
toward our advertised goal of participating in the
revitalization of low-income areas.

Budget's Application Meets Our Financial Criteria

Budget Finance should be able to make payments on schedule.
The anticipated increase in business seems reasonable, given
Budget's strong management and projected market growth.
Drawing on his ten years' experience, Ephram has developed a
program that should attract retailers and overcome the
industry's traditional problems—shoddy merchandise,
inadequate follow-up on defaults, and poor selection of
potential customers. In addition, his bilingual partner and
employees should attract new business in the Spanish-speaking
community.

The retail market in the neighborhoods Budget's retailers
serve is expected to improve as population in the area grows
and as welfare payments and employment increase. Disposable
income in the area should keep pace, justifying Budget's
forecasts.

Although Budget's expenses will be high relative to income
for the next four years (see exhibit 1), these expenditures
will lay the foundation for further income growth. The
installation of computers should help limit the losses
usually associated with the finance business. The proposed
training programs will help retailers improve their business
practices and give company employees the expertise to make
informed decisions and weed out poor prospects. The company's
experienced management, innovative system, and training and
computer programs, combined with a growing economy, should
easily provide Budget with the cash flow necessary to repay
its debt to the bank.

The Loan Will Aid the Minority Community
   This loan will be a visible symbol of the bank's commitment
to helping low-income areas. Budget is involved in almost
every neighborhood in which we have a branch (see exhibit 2).
And, as the company expands, our exposure will also increase.
Joint advertising, both print and TV, will reinforce this
tie. In addition, because the debentures are convertible,
acquiring them will demonstrate the bank's interest in
participating in the ownership of local business.
   Budget's training programs and the loan itself will have a
ripple effect; community retailers will improve their
management skills and Budget will channel the bank's funds to
retailers, indirectly contributing to their increased sales.
   The loan to Budget, then, will serve the bank and the
community.

b.

To: Investment Committee

From: John Lerue

Re: Budget Finance Loan

   Based on my analysis of the Budget Finance Corporation

financial statements, my meetings with Robert Ephram,

Budget's president, and my view of the economic future of New

York, I recommend that we do not purchase the $1.2 million in

convertible debentures. ~~The company's financial record does~~

~~not meet our minimum standards for investment and the loan~~

~~would not meet our objective of aiding the minority~~

~~community.~~

application   *our minimum*

This loan ^application^ does not meet ^our minimum^ ~~normal~~ standards ~~for investment~~

(underlined, not ital.)

has had an unstable

- Budget Finance*'s* income history ~~has been unstable~~

earnings

- The company's ~~income and expense~~ projections are

~~unrealistic~~ *too optimistic*

~~Expense projections are massive~~ *Computerization and training cannot bring in the new business Budget predicts.*

~~Income projections are unrealistic~~

is not strong enough

- Budget*'s* ~~reserves are insufficient~~ to weather any

economic downturn.

Budget's ratio of expenses to income is excessively high.

—Even with ~~this loan, Budget will be~~ *the funds provided by* undercapitalized.

—Although the national economic outlook is excellent,

New York City, particularly the area in which Budget

operates, may not share in this growth and may even

suffer further economic erosion.

- *Management's* ~~Although Budget has an impressive management team, their~~ expertise cannot compensate for the first three

deficiencies.

This loan does not meet our objective of aiding the

minority community.

(underlined, not ital.)

- The Budget system encourages minority residents to purchase shoddy merchandise on credit at inflated prices.
- The $1.2 million could be divided among several ~~better~~ *community* ~~run~~ businesses ~~in the community~~ *that are better risks than Budget.*

--We have *twelve* requests pending.

--We can seek new prospects.

To: Investment Committee
From: John Lerue
Re: Budget Finance Loan

Based on my analysis of the Budget Finance Corporation financial statements, my meetings with Robert Ephram, Budget's president, and my view of the economic future of New York, I recommend that we do not purchase the $1.2 million in convertible debentures.
This loan application does not meet our minimum standards.

- Budget Finance has had an unstable income history.
- The company's earnings projections are too optimistic.
  --Computerization and training cannot bring in the new business Budget predicts.
  --Although the national economic outlook is excellent, New York City, particularly the area in which Budget operates, may not share in this growth and may even suffer further economic erosion.
- Budget is not strong enough to weather an economic downturn.
  --Budget's ratio of expenses to income is excessively high.

--Even with the funds provided by this loan, Budget will
be undercapitalized.
- Although Budget has an impressive management team,
management's expertise cannot compensate for the first
three deficiencies.

This loan does not meet our objective of aiding the
minority community.

- The Budget system encourages minority residents to
purchase shoddy merchandise on credit at inflated
prices.
- The $1.2 million could be divided among several
community businesses that are better risks than Budget.
--We have twelve requests pending.
--We can seek new prospects.

PROBLEM-SOLVING EXAMPLES AND RESEARCH TOOLS

Analysis Tree Exercises

Here are several cases in which managers used analysis trees to be certain they had all the components of a whole or to isolate a problem or opportunity. Each example indicates one way to approach the situation. You might choose another way, but by testing your thinking against another manager's you will become more practiced at using the analysis-tree technique.

Example 1

The president of a construction company involved with the renovation of historically interesting buildings asked his assistant to tell him about the new housing commissioner. The assistant stated the question he thought was really in the president's mind as, "What are the new housing commissioner's views on renovation?" He could not interview the commissioner and had to use secondary sources for information. He decided that if he knew the commissioner's experiences, biases, and knowledge about renovation he might be able to answer the president's question. He therefore put the analysis question "What might indicate the housing commissioner's experience, biases, and knowledge about renovation?" on the left side of the sheet and formed the analysis tree in exhibit A3-1 by asking further questions that might answer the analysis question. How would you develop the tree?

Exhibit A3-1.   Analysis Tree

Question: What are the new housing commissioner's views on renovation?

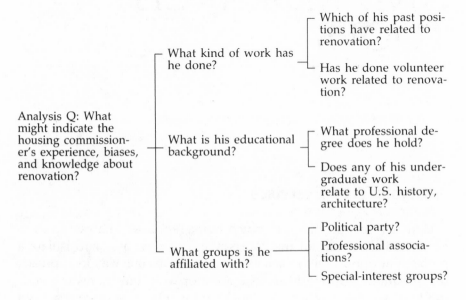

Example 2

The division head of a manufacturing company was asked to evaluate three locations for a small-parts assembly plant. He decided that the decision would be based on the proximity to the company's largest market, the availability of labor, and the costs of operating in each location. A map would indicate proximity to market and census data would indicate whether there was an available labor force, but to determine costs he developed the analysis tree in exhibit A3-2 beginning on the left with this question: "What constitutes cost?" Test your analytical skills against his.

Exhibit A3-2. Analysis Tree

Question: What are the advantages and disadvantages of three possible locations for a small-parts assembly?

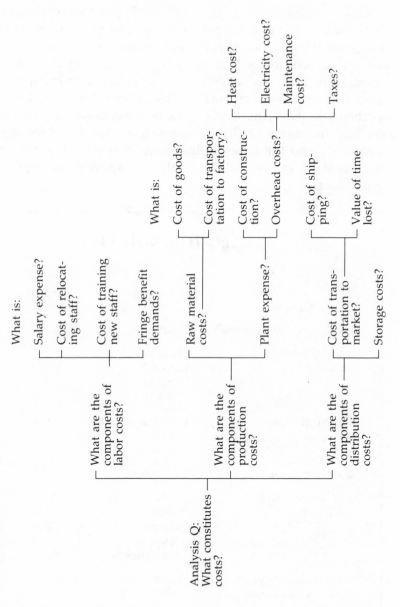

Analysis Q:
What constitutes
costs?

What are the
components of
labor costs?

What is:

Salary expense?

Cost of relocat-
ing staff?

Cost of training
new staff?

Fringe benefit
demands?

What are the
components of
production
costs?

Raw material
costs?

Plant expense?

What is:

Cost of goods?

Cost of transpor-
tation to factory?

Cost of construc-
tion?

Overhead costs?

Heat cost?

Electricity cost?

Maintenance
cost?

Taxes?

What are the
components of
distribution
costs?

Cost of trans-
portation to
market?

Storage costs?

Cost of ship-
ping?

Value of time
lost?

Research Tools

The Need-to-Know List: Primary and Secondary Sources

Once you have developed an analysis tree for complex problems, you know what questions you must answer. A need-to-know list based on the questions on the right-hand side of the tree will focus your research and set up a system for getting the answers you need. You may add questions to your need-to-know list as you continue your research and consider alternatives. For long reports, particularly those involving work by several people, the list should include the name of the person responsible for obtaining the information and the date the information is due. The need-to-know list made by the consultant to the candy manufacturer looked in part like this:

NEED-TO-KNOW-LIST

Question	Possible Sources	Person Responsible	Due Date
Spending on candy down?	Distributors	E.F.	12-1
Candy alternative sales up?	Distributors	E.F.	12-1
	Competitors' annual reports	J.K.	12-4
Candy competitors' sales up?	Competitors' annual reports	J.K.	12-4
New competition?	Distributors	E.F.	12-1
More advertising by competitors?	Marketing manager	A.L.	12-1
	Newspapers, TV, etc.	J.K.	12-4
	Distributors	E.F.	12-1
Lower wholesale prices offered by competitors?	Distributors	E.F.	12-1
Population down? Where?	Census figures	J.K.	12-4

If you organize your research this way, you won't send people scurrying for unnecessary data. There is nothing so annoying to fellow employees as spending several days finding answers to extraneous questions that the researcher later decides he or she really never needed. If you ask for irrelevant data too often, you'll soon find that people don't return your phone calls.

Getting and Organizing Information from Primary Sources. When you list sources on the need-to-know list, remember that your most valuable source of information is other people. An organization is a system made up of complex interrelationships in which much valuable knowledge is never recorded except in the minds of the people who work there. Don't hesitate to ask questions. In seeking the information you need from primary sources, you should keep the following in mind:

- Ask for help and suggestions; people like to be considered experts.
- Consider all sides of the problem, including not only the details on your list, but the context of the organization's objectives and environment as well.
- Seek out both likely and unlikely sources of information: others working on the same problem; predecessors on the job; people with positions similar to yours inside and outside the organization.
- Ask open-ended questions to get all relevant information.
- Ask, "Who else should I talk with?"
- Observe the answerer (not just the answer) for clues to attitudes; observe the situation firsthand if possible.
- For best results, trade information; don't be an interrogator.

Once you've done some fact finding, make sure you store the information appropriately. First, write it down as soon as possible after the meeting. Human memory is notoriously unreliable, and new conversations may cloud your memory of previous talks. Dictating memos for the files is sometimes a useful way to store information, but if you are getting answers for a specific report, you'll be able to retrieve and sort your information more easily if you write it on cards, according to the category you're dealing with.

Here are some simple suggestions for taking notes:

- Put only one important idea on each card.

- Use a number system for sources. Assign a number to each source and write it on a source card, providing enough information to permit you to find the source readily. Then use that number on each research card that provides data from that source.
- File information according to one of the broad categories on the analysis tree.

An information card based on interview data regarding available labor might look like this:

---

3 *(key to source)*   **Labor Costs**

```
Machinists trained in        2,000 in town
   high school:              4,000 in surrounding area


Machinists trained in        500 in town—all working
   trade program:               for Acme Corp.
                             1,000 in area
```

During the fact-finding process, someone may have pointed out a factor you hadn't thought of before. For example, you want to franchise your system for computerized diagnosis of car transmission problems. When you ask potential franchisers, you find that they want maintenance as part of the package. When you talk to Louie Dickson, who's in charge of maintenance, you determine that his people are already overburdened and can't be spared to travel to the franchise shops to provide maintenance. You'll then have to go back to your analysis tree and ask questions about the maintenance problem. As you work, you'll add to both your analysis tree and need-to-know list.

Finding and Organizing Information from Secondary Sources. Even with reams of printed material at their disposal, managers prefer to deal with firsthand information. But it's a mistake to neglect secondary sources, which provide detailed information about the context in which your organization operates. Aggregate data can help you detect significant variations over time that may allow you to zero in on the problem. If you work for a large corporation, you'll probably have access to a company library. If not, you may already have begun building a reference library. Every field has its own journals and books. Appendix 3 gives a list of some of the most helpful reference sources for managers.

Your company files may provide historical insight; at the least, they may provide clues. Sometimes files reveal information buried so deeply in the past that no one around remembers it. Another source is your own file of relevant articles and clippings. Organize these materials according to appropriate categories for the problems you generally deal with so that you do not find yourself searching aimlessly for a *Fortune* article from last spring that you vaguely remember and believe may help you institute the new budget system. One of the values of such secondary sources is that they frequently suggest useful subcategories you can use to group your own thoughts.

However, don't give in to the primeval urge to collect and massage data endlessly in the hope of finding "something." Think first. If you are concerned with the cost of care at a regional hospital that serves a population of 10,000, for example, knowing the cost of care at Bellevue Hospital in New York City will not help you decide what is appropriate for your hospital. When you made your need-to-know list, you set some limits based on your assessment of the reader's needs. As you do the actual research, try to answer the questions on the list to the most practical level and **stop.** If you have done your preparation carefully, and if you don't change your mind about the breadth of the question, you should have enough information.

Once again, use cards to take notes. Be sure to indicate the source so you can double check. For very rich sources, use abbreviations (keep a list so you can remember the abbreviation you use).

Checking for Accuracy and Usefulness. As you collect information, ask yourself two questions:

- Is it accurate?
- Will it help me solve this problem?

If the answer to either is no, forget that morsel of data, no matter how fascinating. Most people are myopic about their environment, and secondary sources may be biased in some direction. It is your responsibility as a writer-researcher to question every source for accuracy.

PRIMARY AND SECONDARY SOURCE CHECKLIST

Ask yourself these questions about your primary sources:

1. Does the source have a vested interest in the result of the study? Will the results directly affect him or her?
2. Does the source have a reputation for accuracy? (We know some managers whose gift for self-promotion tends to get in the way when they are providing information.)

Ask yourself these questions as you read your secondary sources:

1. Is the source objective? (Are there any obvious biases?)
2. Is the source up to date?
3. Are statistical sources comparable? (It may be impossible to use two sets of statistical data to support your argument because they were developed on the basis of different samples or used different methods. Check for this before you actually begin to write your report.)

INDEX

Page numbers in *italics* refer to figures.

<u>WEDNES 10:00</u>

- Come-up w/ more ? for kids assessment
- bring in paper
- look at my stuff to add to program